Committing TO THE CULTURE

Committing TO THE CULTURE

How Leaders Can Create and Sustain Positive Schools

STEVE GRUENERT
TODD WHITAKER

ASCD

Alexandria, Virginia USA

1703 N. Beauregard St. • Alexandria, VA 22311-1714 USA
Phone: 800-933-2723 or 703-578-9600 • Fax: 703-575-5400
Website: www.ascd.org • E-mail: member@ascd.org
Author guidelines: www.ascd.org/write

Ronn Nozoe, *Interim CEO & Executive Director;* Stefani Roth, *Publisher;* Genny Ostertag, *Director, Content Acquisitions;* Susan Hills, *Acquisitions Editor;* Julie Houtz, *Director, Book Editing & Production;* Miriam Calderone, *Editor;* Judi Connelly, *Senior Art Director;* Donald Ely, *Associate Art Director;* Cynthia Stock, *Typesetter;* Trinay Blake, *E-Publishing Specialist;* Kelly Marshall, *Interim Manager, Production Services*

All web links in this book are correct as of the publication date below but may have become inactive or otherwise modified since that time. If you notice a deactivated or changed link, please e-mail books@ascd.org with the words "Link Update" in the subject line. In your message, please specify the web link, the book title, and the page number on which the link appears.

PAPERBACK ISBN: 978-1-4166-2784-5   ASCD product #119007   n6/19
PDF E-BOOK ISBN: 978-1-4166-2786-9; see Books in Print for other formats.
Quantity discounts are available: e-mail programteam@ascd.org or call 800-933-2723, ext. 5773, or 703-575-5773. For desk copies, go to www.ascd.org/deskcopy.

Library of Congress Cataloging-in-Publication Data is available for this title.
LCCN: 2019013196

27 26 25 24 23 22 21 20 19   1 2 3 4 5 6 7 8 9 10 11 12

Committing TO THE CULTURE

How Leaders Can Create and Sustain Positive Schools

Acknowledgments

This is the third book I have written with Todd Whitaker. I have known and worked with him for nearly 20 years now, and it would be silly for me to think any of these books could be successful without him. The world knows Todd is a very smart guy, and I know how goofy he is, which makes all this stuff possible. Thanks, Todd!

—Steve Gruenert

Steve Gruenert is the most knowledgeable person there is regarding educational culture, and I feel fortunate that he has brought me along on his journey to positively inform educators and influence cultures in schools. It has been a pleasure and an honor.

—Todd Whitaker

Introduction

Culture is a broad, complex concept that can mean different things to different people. One way we think of a school's culture is as the personality of the building. Organizational culture expert Edgar Schein notes that all people are "a conglomerate of the beliefs and values of the groups they were members of. . . . [W]hen these beliefs and values are basically the same for a bunch of people, the term *culture* becomes a convenient word" to describe that convergence (personal communication, Jan. 31, 2019). Culture is *who we are*, not *what we have*. This is why it is difficult to change.

Another way we think of culture is as information passed from one generation to the next explaining how to survive the environment. When the environment changes, some of this information can become obsolete. Yet—perhaps out of pride, ego, or the wish to prevent the younger generation from making the same mistakes they did—the older folks keep pressing what they learned, even if it is no longer relevant or helpful.

As we dig deeper into the concept of culture, we find that the stories told and the language used among a group of people convey their collective values and beliefs; they are the conduits and, eventually, the vehicles of change. In positive school cultures, the stories told by administrators, teachers, and support staff revolve around what has worked to support student success. In toxic schools—which may look similar to positive schools in at least some respects—the stories being told are more about survival, what does not work around here, and how the lack of support from outside the school has forced members of the culture to become stronger (in the wrong ways). School leaders who seek to shift their toxic culture to a more positive culture will be more successful when they address the stories being told.

In this book, we aim to provide school leaders with ideas for shifting their cultures to be more positive and supportive of those who wish to become the best they can be. Keep in mind that tackling school culture means you are *going for it*. You are not looking for behavioral compliance from faculty and staff; you are reaching for every ounce of commitment they have to give. If that level of commitment is not your goal, then you might consider leaving culture alone for now and beginning with shifting attitudes or the school climate. There is nothing wrong with focusing on the climate, at least initially, but keep in mind that eventually, all roads lead to the culture.

Why Is the Building-Level Culture So Important?

There are many layers of culture in education: the classroom, the building, the district, the state, and the nation. In this book, we focus on the building layer of culture because it has the greatest effect on student achievement and overall school performance.

Why not the other layers? First, the classroom layer is too narrow, and class composition usually changes from year to year; it's less a culture than a community of learners, without the intense ownership that comes when we invest our identity into a group. And the district, state, and national layers are too broad. Although all the schools in a given district are overseen by a single school board that provides policies, financial support, and other resources, the board's influence on school culture is not as strong as you might think. Visit any two schools within a school district and you'll see what we mean. They may have the same grade levels, serve the same community, receive the same funding, and teach the same curriculum, but they will be very different in how they "do" education. Similarly, the state and national layers affect funding and influence what can or cannot be done in schools, but whatever "speed limit" they try to impose, each school will have its own flow of traffic.

Which brings us back to the building layer. Here's a step-by-step look at how the culture of the school building ultimately affects student achievement:

- The school culture determines the types of conversations faculty members have.
- Faculty conversations determine the level of faculty commitment.
- Faculty commitment leverages faculty efficacy.
- Faculty efficacy affects individual teacher efficacy.
- Individual teacher efficacy affects the quality of instructional delivery.
- The quality of instructional delivery affects student efficacy.
- Student efficacy drives student academic performance and behavior in the classroom.

What's in This Book

Before plunging in, it's important to be aware of two facts about culture. First, we rarely, if ever, start at zero when we set out to build or transform school culture. Where there are people hanging around one another for a significant period, there is a culture.

Second, whenever we try to shape a new culture, we take pieces of the old one with us. The emerging culture will inevitably be a hybrid that blends successes and challenges of the past with visions of the future. Before any of us became school employees, we attended school. Some of us never quit attending school. And all of us bring our experiences and dispositions with us to the next setting. If the new culture is too distant from the old one, we may struggle to find an identity—our social home.

The deep commitment required to make significant cultural shifts, coupled with our tendency to cling to the past and bring pieces of it wherever we go, may help us understand why cultures can be so resistant to lasting change. In this book, we unpack these and other questions around what inhibits and what fosters sustainable culture change that withstands fads, toxic mindsets, and other threats.

We begin in Chapter 1 by exploring deep questions around the nature of culture, including the importance of vision and climate and how the tension between the past and the future can keep a culture stagnant. In Chapter 2, we examine the factors that contribute to stubborn toxic cultures, how *not* to change those cultures, and whether your school culture needs to change. In Chapter 3, we discuss how to create positive culture change through trust, collaboration, and commitment rather than fear, competition, and compliance. Finally, in Chapter 4, we offer advice on the difficult task of ensuring sustained culture change.

Throughout the book, we provide scenarios drawing from our own experiences in schools, although names have been changed. We hope these vignettes give some sense of how our ideas and approaches work in practice and demonstrate that every school has stumbling blocks along with successes on the journey to culture change. We're all in this together. Now let's get started!

1

Gaining a Deeper Understanding of Culture

In this chapter, we explore deep questions around the nature of culture, including what culture reflects and how our own mindsets affect our perception of it; how factors such as vision and climate shape a culture; the influence of various roles in the culture "movie"; and how the tension between the past and the future can keep a culture stagnant.

Culture as a Reflection of the Leader

We believe that it takes five years to change a culture, for better or worse. After five years, the culture is more a reflection of the leader than anything else. Figure 1.1 summarizes the priorities of both effective and ineffective principals over a five-year period—and the cultures that result.

Our encapsulation of what ineffective principals do year after year may seem harsh, but we have seen it happen. It does not take much effort to build a toxic culture. Research tells us that if a leader does nothing, or does the same ineffective things year after year, the

FIGURE 1.1

Effective Principals Versus Ineffective Principals

	Effective Principal	**Ineffective Principal**
Year 1	• Wandering • Listening • Asking relevant questions • Challenging irrelevant egos • Relating	• Wandering • Mandating • Avoiding • Reacting
Year 2	• Listening • Asking relevant questions • Relating • Empowering • Dreaming	• Wandering • Mandating • Avoiding • Reacting
Year 3	• Listening • Cultivating • Dividing • Observing	• Wandering • Mandating • Avoiding • Reacting
Year 4	• Recruiting • Supporting • Branding	• Wandering • Mandating • Avoiding • Reacting
Year 5	• Solidifying • Celebrating • Listening	• Wandering • Mandating • Avoiding • Reacting
Outcome	A positive school culture that attracts effective educators	A toxic school culture that recruits and rewards ineffective educators

school's culture will drift toward negativity (Deal & Peterson, 2010). And some ineffective principals may put a lot of energy toward what they think is good management when they are actually building a wall, with them on the outside. We envision this wall much like the fourth wall in theater, which separates the actor and the audience. Some prefer to have the wall quite thick to create distance between them and those watching, whereas others break down the wall so that they can connect with the audience. When school leaders are experiencing stress, they may create such a boundary in an effort to hide their vulnerability. Paradoxically, however, this wall is not protective. If a school leader has walled herself off from staff during stressful times, she may find that she no longer has the trust of the faculty and staff and, in dire cases, may be seen as the enemy.

Let's go through the years summarized in Figure 1.1:

- *Year one:* The concept of "leadership by wandering around," introduced in the 1990s, means simply leaving one's office and wandering around the school, engaging with staff through such interactions as spontaneous classroom visits and short conversations with the goal of strengthening relationships, professional practice, and culture. Although we are not discounting this approach, what principals do while they're wandering counts for a lot. Note how the priorities of effective and ineffective leaders diverge after that initial "wandering." Some principals wander for years on end with no purpose, creating a mere illusion of leadership.

- *Year two:* It's not by chance that after year one, effective leaders shift their focus from wandering to more targeted actions, including listening, recruiting, and supporting. They become more purposeful in determining the strategic people as well as the strategic issues. At this point, the honeymoon is over, and any resistance will get real. Ineffective leaders will continue to wander in year two, avoiding conflict while making a show of being connected.

- *Year three:* By this time, an effective principal knows which teachers represent the future of the school and which do not. A key priority here is *dividing*. Think of the dividing process as placing all irrelevant opinions and egos on an island where they can do little damage. This is a social division: the leader separates those who want to improve from those who are stuck in the past, thereby preventing the latter from negatively influencing the good things happening at the school.

- *Year four:* This year is critical, because many school leaders may get complacent, thinking everything is in place after three years of effort. But for the new culture to stick, it will need at least two years (years four and five) of continued effort. This is where some leaders may run out of commitment, change jobs, retire, or get promoted. Year four is often the time when a new culture loses its grip. The ineffective leader will assume year four is a done deal (that is, if he or she gets to year four). Effective leaders continue their push by recruiting and supporting effective, positive staff members.
- *Year five:* Although you don't need to wait until year five to celebrate, this is a good time to solidify what you've put in place. We encourage all leaders to celebrate any progress being made—including the small, easy wins—as they evolve into a better school. Celebrating progress in a purposeful and meaningful way in year five strengthens the culture and makes it resilient to negativity.

Culture: Something We *Have* or Something We *Are?*

Some people believe school culture is something they *have* rather than something they *are* (Geertz, 1973). This distinction may initially seem purely semantic, but when we dig deeper, we see that it indicates a significant difference in mindset. When you imagine culture as something you *have,* you're making it something that can be set aside or changed without letting it influence what you do or how you think. By contrast, seeing culture as something you *are* makes it much more indelible and difficult to deny or change.

Anthropologist Edward T. Hall (1990) wrote, "Anthropologists have known for a long time that all aspects of a culture are interrelated. They also know that to change one thing is to change everything" (p. 196). Think of an ecosystem, with its countless interdependent parts. Similarly, anthropologists and ethnographers describe culture as something in our heads that provides "programming" as we decode our environments (Hofstede, Hofstede, & Minkov, 2010; Schein & Schein, 2017). Whatever new things show up will be interpreted through the existing program.

Whatever metaphor we use to define culture, the meaning is clear: cultures are large and complex, and you can't just make a superficial improvement and expect the larger culture to shift. Those who envision changing their culture quickly and easily believe that school culture is something they *have* and can switch out like a pair of shoes—that once they grow tired of it, they can simply set it down and move on to the next idea. We warn against adopting this mindset, which will ultimately drive you in circles, going nowhere fast. You will be more productive if you see culture as something you *are* and work to change it slowly and holistically, from the inside out.

Shaping the Culture: Illusion Versus Vision

Culture can be shaped by illusion or vision. An illusion is something our minds project onto reality. Illusions can make our brand of reality a bit more tolerable and fool us into thinking everything is OK.

Sometimes the culture builds an edifice of illusions to convince a group of people that certain beliefs and behaviors are necessary to improve, or even to survive.

Whenever any group of people hangs together for a long period of time, a culture will evolve. We are hardwired to form connections with others. If the family, church, or school does not meet this need, then perhaps a gang, a cult, or a social network will. Whatever group we decide to identify with determines who we are, who the enemy is, and what is true. Each group we join will have its own "movie," and we will seek out our roles in that movie. Most of us think the old movies are the best; most of us think the old ways are still relevant.

Look around your classroom or school building. Does the place look like it did 30 years ago? The world of education is steeped in tradition that is difficult to uproot. Research continually reveals new cognitive breakthroughs in learning, yet we still put chairs in rows, lecture students, and wait for the bells. Alumni want their children to receive the same education they did. A vision for a new and better future is often held in check by the illusions advocated by the current culture.

Why do most school cultures sell a future that looks like the current one? It's not because they are bent on sabotage. Quite the opposite: the purpose of culture is to survive the future by sharing stories of those who have survived the past. Most cultures are trying to prevent people from stepping out into traffic.

But it's important to take risks and step into the unknown. No matter how great a school is now, it can't move forward if it doesn't have a vision of a better future, something to move toward. A vision is really a conversation people have about what they hope the future will hold. A clear vision strips away the illusions of the current culture, serving as an antidote to the subtle slide back into old ways.

Climate: A Window into the Culture

Let's look at the role of climate, which is often conflated with culture. They are not the same thing, but they are connected. Climate is an indicator of how things are; it's the way most people feel on a normal day. These feelings generally arise in response to an external stimulus, such as an event, the day of the week, or even the weather. By contrast, "[c]ulture is the personality of the building. It is the professional religion of the group. Culture gives permission to climate to act as it does" (Gruenert & Whitaker, 2017, pp. 3–4). If something happens once, it affects the climate. If it happens all the time, it becomes part of the culture. Simply put, climate reveals the culture.

Most school climates have a consistency about them. When something happens, we can usually predict how people will feel about it. If the fire alarm sounds, students may smile and prepare to visit with friends outside, while teachers feel frustrated by the interruption to their lesson. Each group is simply responding as the culture has taught it to.

When a school is improving, the climate feels different. There is a sense of hope and anticipation. The trivial things that usually bother us don't seem as important when we can sense something better around the corner. When the school is improving, people become more patient, more forgiving. There is more humor, and mistakes are not morale killers. People want to be there. We can tell how well a school is doing by the complaints we hear. If people are complaining about the weather or a baseball team, the school is probably in good shape.

Climate can also tell us when we are heading toward a negative place. Trivial issues seem to provoke big discussions. People vent about issues that should not be issues, such as lukewarm pizza in the cafeteria or kids wearing hats in school. If the leadership does nothing about it, frustration will eventually create fissures along social lines, and negative conversations will build into a confederacy. Minor gripes can become building-level issues if the culture is in a bad place.

The building-level climate is the most revealing element of culture when looking for clues as to which direction the school is heading. When school leaders set out to shift the school's culture, they can peek at the climate to see whether they are improving things or just frustrating people.

Let's look at a scenario that illustrates this. When Ms. Garcia, a principal we once worked with, returned from a national conference, she wanted to share a few ideas with her staff, including having teachers engage in nonevaluative observations of one another's teaching. At the next faculty meeting, she shared a few ways other schools were doing it and, hoping a few teachers might give it a try, asked for volunteers. Several raised their hands.

Ms. Garcia invited the volunteers to take the lead in developing their own protocols, scheduling the observations, engaging in discussion prior to or after the observations, coming up with "look-fors," determining the duration of the observations, and so on. She wanted them to own the process and to have a chance to be creative. Then she left them alone. She wanted to let the climate inform her as to whether this was a good idea, so she observed the feelings of all the adults in the building—not just the teachers doing observations.

Were they talking about it informally? Did it seem frustrating to make the schedules work? Were more teachers getting involved? Was the culture pushing back?

It did not take long for good news to travel back to Ms. Garcia. To her surprise, by the time she heard the experiment was doing well, she discovered that a few additional teachers had joined in. She was especially gratified when one of her average teachers came to her in the hallway to express her appreciation for how a few teachers were taking time to help her—not realizing it was the principal who had made it happen. And Ms. Garcia wanted it that way. There was no need to discuss it during faculty meetings or to post the news in the school's *Friday Focus*—not yet. To use the culture as the conduit for this initiative, it needed to be shared by word of mouth. In a true collaborative culture, the stories teachers tell other teachers become the foundation of improvement. In this setting, the climate revealed ample satisfaction among faculty who were engaged in this project.

This is how the climate of the school can be the window into the culture. When we want something new to become part of the culture, we cannot force it with a mandate or even a preselected set of procedures. Instead, we need to quietly plant it among the (more effective) staff members and let them run with it. If it works, they will take it beyond our dreams. If it does not work, it may have been a bad time to start, or maybe it was too much, too soon. Maybe it just wasn't a good idea.

And be patient: bringing in donuts on Friday may lead to a temporary positive spike in the climate, but only doing something repeatedly over a long period of time will make it part of the culture. You'll know it's become part of the culture when nobody notices it anymore.

Playing the Part: The Influence of Roles on School Culture

We often use the analogy of a movie to help folks understand the concept of school culture. We are always auditioning for the next movie; the question is, what role will we play?

Every teacher a school hires has hopes of becoming one of the best teachers in that school. No doubt the administration also hopes for this outcome. However, most new teachers end up being average, and some below average. It's never anyone's plan to become a weak teacher, but it happens. It may seem counterintuitive, but weak teachers often have roles to play in the school culture.

One paper on this topic (Gruenert & McDaniel, 2009) suggests that many of the weak teachers we wish we could get rid of never wanted to be that way; they simply landed in a negative role that existed in the school's movie. Most movies need "bad guys" for dramatic tension, after all. Instead of firing the bad guys, we recommend changing the roles in the school's movie so bad guys don't exist. Treat the weak or negative teachers as if they still had a desire to be effective teachers, and get rid of the rewards that keep the bad guys hanging around. The trick is to coax them out of their negative roles and into more positive roles. This can't be done in a toxic school culture, which will try to convince you the current movie is pretty good.

Before we elaborate on the negative roles some teachers play, let's look at some of the positive roles we find in more effective schools. A good school may not have all these roles filled, but chances are, as you read each description, certain faces will come to mind:

- *The worker* is the teacher who has the unmatched work ethic. This does not always translate as being the teacher who arrives early and leaves late; rather, she is constantly thinking about what could be improved, experimenting with new strategies, running to share ideas with others, and writing down things on whatever paper is available. This teacher cannot get enough learning.
- *The supporter* is the teacher who is motivated by helping others, even those who tend to be negative. He may be that teacher who is always willing to hang around a few extra minutes to make sure a student's parents show up or who smiles when a colleague has made a great presentation to the staff.
- *The hero* is the teacher who is able to minimize the influence of negative or toxic teachers. She may be the teacher who makes eye contact with a negative teacher just before he has a negative outburst, using that body language to keep it from happening. We don't often see heroes at work, but we know who they are and can feel the "social security" they provide.

This is just a sampling of the many positive roles teachers may play in schools. These people exist because the culture values them, and their colleagues believe they are needed. In the best cultures, these roles can be played by many teachers, not just one or two.

Now let's look at some of the roles that ineffective teachers may own. These are the people who benefit from a school culture that resists change. These are weak teachers who have found support for their character in the school's movie:

- *The social director* is the teacher who makes sure everyone is having a good time. Despite her weak performance as a teacher, she makes herself valuable by bringing in food, handing out birthday cards, asking about people's families, sympathizing with anyone who is having a hard time, and coordinating social events. The social director knows she is a weak teacher, so she builds a support group of connected people (e.g., support staff, veteran faculty, parents, board members) to bolster her when teacher evaluations come around.

- *The joker* is the teacher who discovered early on that making colleagues laugh is a quick way of getting validation. He always has a joke ready at any formal or informal gathering, sometimes with inappropriate subject matter. He finds faults in others and laughs at their miscues. He has found that being the comedian helps him avoid the discomfort of being found out as a weak teacher.

- *The informant* is the teacher who feels the need to keep everyone in every loop. He shares many stories throughout the day; whether there is any truth behind these stories is irrelevant. He describes incidents, situations, and mistakes made by others to anyone who will listen. His storytelling is also available to anyone in the community who craves inside information about who is doing what in the school building. Being perceived as a resource for crucial information is the cushion that absorbs much criticism of his weak teaching.

- *The hometown star* is the beloved teacher or coach who grew up in the community, attended the school, won awards, and provided the community with countless highlights back in the day. She tells great stories and enjoys a certain celebrity status. The school still displays trophies of her accomplishments, and stories of her rise to stardom abound. Because people in the school and community want to be associated with her, she can do no wrong, even when her teaching is not up to par.

Let's look at how someone might fall into one of these roles. Imagine a new teacher who seeks validation from veteran teachers. He looks for ways to please these veterans and finds he can make them laugh, which makes him feel like part of the family. This role as entertainer sticks, and soon it's the character other teachers expect him to be—sometimes to the detriment of his teaching. He may relish the role and its accolades to the point of forsaking the real reason he was hired.

Can you think of any teachers in your school who are less than effective but are protected for reasons that have nothing to do with their teaching? They might be playing one of the roles we described. Again, the goal is not to fire these teachers but to get rid of the negative characters in the movie. Change the script these teachers have been carrying around.

In one school we worked with, the principal began to notice in her second year that a handful of veteran teachers who did not do much were held in high esteem by the faculty and the community. They showed up at school just in time to get their first classes going and managed to follow the buses out of the parking lot every afternoon. In class, they kept the students quiet and busy but did little teaching. They seemed confident—and protected.

To this principal, it seemed that any sudden move by the administration to challenge these teachers would have been a mistake. We wondered if teachers' primary goal in this school was to achieve the status that allowed them to come and go as they pleased, with nobody bothering them in the classroom—call it "autonomy." If that was true, it was because the culture supported this reward. To reach this level and behave in such a way may have been a sign of prestige in this school.

The principal did not intend to let this state of affairs continue, but, rather than confronting these people, she let the culture do most of the work. We have found that leaders often try to do too much when they already have a support system in place—the social network. Some of the veteran teachers at this school did not support this type of behavior and were more than willing to discuss with the principal where they believed it all started and who the "champions" of this negative behavior were. During the course of these informal discussions, the principal gradually gave these veteran teachers permission to challenge the negative behaviors of a few teachers.

You may be wondering what this looked like. Did the veteran teachers take the lazy, negative teachers out back and beat them up? Did they slash their tires? Nope. They started by identifying the negative teacher least committed to behaving this way and invited him to hang out with them. They befriended this teacher and began to dominate the time when he would normally be hanging out with the other negative teachers, creating a social distance between him and the rest of the bunch. Eventually, this "converted" teacher helped recruit the second-least committed negative teacher. In the end, there weren't many teachers left in the negative group, and it was no longer cool to act the way they did.

People in negative roles will begin to form excuses early in the school year (or in their career) to evade responsibility for their performance and reject any label of ineffectiveness that tries to stick to them. These excuses might include the following:

- "I am too busy."
- "The principal is not fair."
- "I've tried that many times, and it never works."
- "I've done it this way many times, and it always works."
- "These students don't care."
- "I have a dentist appointment that day."
- "It's not my fault."

Remember, these quotes are found in the movie script; they are not unique to the actors. If you remove these people, the roles may remain, waiting for others to fill them. Even if most of these teachers leave, their stories will still be lingering in the hallways, the lounge, or the parking lot. Other teachers will remember and seek the rewards that incentivized those past teachers' ineffectiveness. A new teacher might hear stories and ask, "Is this true? Can we do this here?" School leaders who seek to build a stronger, positive culture will need to identify these roles because the existing culture will try to find a way to keep the story alive and the roles the same.

Can Stability Be a Bad Thing?

We have established that cultures work hard to maintain the status quo. This is partly because everyone has an internal voice that guards the future by using the past as the sole reference point in decision making. We call this voice the *guardian of the past*. Guardian of the past can also be a role taken on by people in the school who are skeptical of change and work to ensure the positive legacy of the school lives on by using the past as a framework. The future is the most uncertain of all places, while the past is the most certain. Thus, when a group needs to make a difficult or unprecedented decision, it will often search the past for a solution. Whatever happens next needs to look like something that has already happened. Predictability equals stability.

Is it such a bad thing that cultures reward stability? For some, this internal voice helps them find ways to make their jobs easier. For example, some teachers may find that intentionally fostering negative student attitudes by doing unpopular things such as giving frequent pop quizzes makes life easier by increasing the distance between the teacher and students. If students are unhappy with you, you don't have to invest any emotions in relationships with them. Other teachers may find that fostering positive student attitudes in an ineffective way makes it easier to do their jobs—for example, by being an easy grader or overly permissive with behaviors. What kid would not want to be in a class with a teacher who wanted to be friends with his students or avoid conflict at all costs? Imagine coming to school knowing that you can talk your teacher out of any difficult assignments! If either of these two approaches is part of the culture, then it will be the easiest thing to do, and there are unwritten rewards waiting to honor this behavior.

The guardian of the past will determine which part of the past we may use to inform future actions. This voice will remind people what they have done in the past and whether repeating it or doing something different would be better. As we'll see in Chapter 4, guardians of the past often have the same interest as those seeking change; they just need to understand the benefits of occasional instability, which can provide an opportunity to shape a new culture for the better. Leaders who are aware of the guardian voice can use it to support what the school needs to do to improve.

One of the biggest threats a change in the culture can bring is a change in how people socialize. As Grenny and colleagues (Grenny, Patterson, Maxfield, McMillan, & Switzer, 2013) note, "When breaking away from habits that are continually reinforced by a person's existing social network, people must be plucked from their support structure and placed in a new network" (p. 164). It may be necessary to think about ways to change some structures in the current system as a means to reshuffle the social deck, such as changing planning times, reassigning special duties, or rebuilding committees. By doing so, you can create distance between effective teachers and toxic teachers. We have been asked in the past whether pairing good teachers with ineffective teachers can "fix" the latter, but there is way too much uncertainty in that equation to guarantee positive results.

Summing Up

In this chapter, we looked at culture through a variety of lenses. We hope you formed a deeper understanding of culture that will enable you to create culture change with greater authority and productivity and much less frustration.

Change can be scary; to change a culture is to change a part of the organization's personality. But change can also be invigorating, driving people to work together to solve new problems, build new relationships, and even make new mistakes.

Positive cultures value mistakes for the learning and growth they impart. By contrast, toxic cultures attempt to obstruct change and hide mistakes at all costs. In the next chapter, we'll look at how toxic cultures are formed and why they're so difficult to shift.

2

Toxic School Cultures: How They Get That Way and Stay That Way

One of the toughest and most common obstacles school leaders face on the road to improvement is toxic culture. Before we explore what creates the stubborn toxicity we see in so many school cultures, let's take a moment to distinguish *toxic* school cultures from *negative* school cultures. In many schools, these terms are used interchangeably, as if being negative were a form of being toxic. But they are not the same thing, and once we understand the difference, we will be able to approach the challenges each raises more effectively.

Teachers who are *negative* always seem to be pushing back on new ideas and innovations. Although they are committed to student performance and want the school to be seen as successful in the eyes of the community, they tend to be stubborn and unwilling to change.

By contrast, a *toxic* teacher leads other teachers into a collective mindset of disloyalty to the school mission, irreverence for students and parents, and a posture of self-defense whenever improvement is mentioned. Unlike negative teachers, toxic teachers are committed only to themselves and to surviving the next new idea or initiative.

Toxic teachers have a spiteful mindset, whispering in others' ears throughout the school and community that the only way to survive this miserable place is to join their gang. Thus, all toxic teachers are negative, but not all negative teachers are toxic.

In this chapter, we explore how a toxic culture is formed, what *not* to do when trying to transform the culture, and how to tell whether a culture truly needs changing.

How a Toxic Culture Is Formed

The following scenario illustrates how a toxic culture can come about.

It's the beginning of the school year, and at the first faculty meeting, the new principal introduces the idea of incorporating Positive Behavioral Interventions and Supports (PBIS) into the system. During the break, a few teachers gather in the hallway to talk about PBIS. A first-year teacher is standing nearby pretending to be texting but really listening. The conversation goes like this:

> **Teacher 1:** What are your thoughts about that new PBIS deal? It sounds like it might be a lot of work. We have plenty of students who don't behave, but why should *we* have to change? Why shouldn't the students prove to us that they have the ability to do the right thing, and then we can go from there? If the administration just followed the current discipline policy and put the hammer down more often, maybe we wouldn't need to adjust how we do things.

> **Teacher 2:** To me, it sounds like the same old, same old. It's just the latest trend that will disappear like the last dozen. If we just wait out the new know-it-all principal, she'll be gone like the last few. You're right—principals need to enforce

the rules, not make new ones that force us to change. In the old days, if students even looked cross-eyed at a teacher, the principal would boot them out and the parents would give them a boot at home. That's what we need, not some newfangled, touchy-feely participation-trophy approach. If we all refuse to do it, or just ignore it, what are they going to do to us?

Can you identify which teacher is negative and which is toxic? Teacher 1 is using the past as a reason to be cautious, whereas Teacher 2 is using the past as a weapon. Teacher 2 is recruiting, and if he's able to raise sufficient troops, a subcultural army could form, giving rise to a toxic new school culture.

Subcultures often emerge when teachers come together to address shared issues. If the administration is unable to relieve teachers' discomfort with a given issue, a group of teachers will form to deal with the issue in their own way. Here is the conversation Teacher 2 uses to pull in two new teachers the next day:

> **Teacher 2:** Hi. How are you newbies doing? Kids driving you crazy yet? We have some doozies this year, for sure.
>
> **New Teacher A:** Most of my day goes OK, but right after lunch and the last hour of the day wear me out. Teaching is a lot harder than I thought it would be!
>
> **Teacher 2:** Just wait. It gets worse, not better. Have you been in the cafeteria? It's like a zoo without a zookeeper in there. We used to have assigned seats and no talking, but this new-age principal believes in the inmates running the asylum. That's why the students are out of control after lunch. It didn't use to be like that at all. They'd march in and out like soldiers.

New Teacher B: The first week of school was all right, but it seems like the students are less respectful now. I'm not sure what I should do to calm my class down.

Teacher 2: There is really nothing you can do. Until the boss in the office cracks down on the bad eggs, you just have to ride it out and hope some of them are absent come cold and flu season. Of course, those are always the kids with perfect attendance. Ugh!

The two new teachers listen wide-eyed as their confidence is further chipped away. Their shoulders start to droop.

Teacher 2: If you think things are bad now, did you hear that nonsense about a new PBIS program the principal wants *us* to implement? I guarantee it will wear you out even more. Additional responsibilities for the teachers, fewer responsibilities for the office—just the way they like it. The office already does nothing when you send a mouthy brat their way. Now you're supposed to keep that mouthy brat in your classroom and work to help them "de-escalate" and "learn self-control." Ha! I can tell you this: to me, PBIS stands for a Pretty Bad Idea that Sucks.

As this small group of teachers continues to meet informally, they form a bond. Talking about possible responses to this crazy idea momentarily eases their discomfort. It feels good to gather with comrades to discuss offensive or defensive moves. These meetings may become exclusive and secret. Eventually, it becomes clear that the goal is not to address challenges associated with using PBIS, but to assuage teachers' discomfort with the change foisted upon them. The informal meetings and winks or nods in public places provide relief and bind the teachers as a family. This approach becomes the solution to most problems they face in the future. And just like that, a toxic culture is born.

The Illusion of Effectiveness

If toxic cultures can spring up so easily, why can't they be uprooted easily? Well, if teachers like Teacher 2 have enough influence, they can immerse us in a toxic narrative that taints every part of our daily experience to the extent that we don't even realize we're in it. And some teachers can create an illusion of effectiveness when, in reality, they are not at all effective. They are part of the reason why toxic cultures are so stubborn. These players navigate their cultures expertly, subtly securing a place for themselves amid change by only appearing to make a positive impact.

That illusion they create is key. Think about it: in our society, we invest in items that we believe will make us look thinner, stronger, smarter, richer, younger, or more attractive. Creating these illusions provides a sense of confidence that aligns with the expectations of society. In Cialdini's (2018) work about the power of influence and the science of *pre-suasion*—that is, the act of preparing people to be receptive to a message before they receive it—he shares how people create illusions to convince others to behave a certain way. The following six "weapons" of influence can create conditions to affect the realities of others:

- *Social proof:* Everybody else is doing it, so we should, too.
- *Consistency:* We have always done it this way.
- *Reciprocity:* If we do them a favor, they will owe us a favor.
- *Scarcity:* Because we are the only ones able to do this, they will have to leave us alone.

- *Liking:* If we can be friends, their expectations of us may relax.
- *Authority:* If we are perceived to be experts or authorities, others will listen to us.

Authority is not as commonly used by teachers as the others, so we will limit the scope of our discussion to the first five weapons. Let's look at how these weapons are deployed in classrooms where everything seems to be in place yet students learn very little. The culture knows it. The culture allows it.

Social proof. Here we find a few weak teachers using the crowd as a shield. If an issue is raised or teachers' practice is questioned, a typical response is "Other teachers are doing the same thing, so why target me?" The weight of the group seems to give the practice validity.

These teachers may use an anecdotal approach to shore up their case—for example, pointing out that one or two of the "untouchable" teachers also rely heavily on lecture. This is a case of misdirection: it isn't the strategy that is necessarily the problem, but the teachers' ineffectiveness in implementing the strategy. The teacher who uses social proof is expert at storytelling, using facts to lend legitimacy to his or her argument and convert excuses into reasons. Focusing on the results rather than the approach is one way to redirect the conversation to the real problem.

Consistency. This approach finds teachers using the successes of the past as the reason they are still doing the same thing 20 years later. Whereas social proof is about everyone doing it now, consistency is about everyone doing it way back when—so let's keep doing it.

Faculty in a school with predominantly high-socioeconomic-status (SES) students can be especially resistant to change because test scores and other traditional measures are more likely to show "success" than they are at schools with lower-SES populations. In these schools, teachers can hide behind the students. Most of the time, the "good old days" were not really that good, but when a person has a long history of success, his or her anecdotal examples can seem very powerful. In such cases, the change effort should focus not on whether teachers' practice is good enough, but on whether they are doing the best they can do. Making that shift in mindset can have a significant influence on a culture stuck in the past.

Reciprocity. Some teachers believe that if they provide services to others, they may not be evaluated strictly. If they bring brownies to a professional learning community (PLC) meeting, people might not notice or care about their lack of teaching skill. Every school has at least one teacher who may not be effective but is always willing to help, offer tips, or do favors, such as volunteering for unpopular activities or committees, covering classes for colleagues, or sharing lesson plans. If the teacher can accumulate enough favors from enough people, his or her ability to teach may become secondary, if not overlooked altogether.

There are myriad examples of this. The 57-year-old ex-quarterback who has been ineffective in the classroom for years may offer to leverage community sentiment or sway a board member who used to play on his team in exchange for favors from others in the building. It's hard not to go easy on the teacher who wrote you a heartfelt note when your cat died, compliments your teaching (without ever observing you), or offers to watch a class for you when you appear to be tired or busy. A successful extracurricular coach or cheerleader sponsor may get away with being less energetic or effective in the classroom or rarely serving on committees—and when they do attend a meeting, they make sure to let you know that you're imposing on their personal agendas and owe them one.

Cialdini (2018) reminds us that nobody likes owing anyone a favor, and sometimes we go to excessive lengths to repay a favor just so we can wipe the slate clean. Reciprocity works best when the one deploying it as a weapon is subtle about it. Teachers using this weapon may give the impression that they are providing a public service, only to remind you later of their generosity when they need something from you. One way to thwart this tactic is to thank them immediately for whatever service they provided, preventing them from depositing it into their "favors" account.

Scarcity. People who are able to provide a rare service may try to leverage that scarcity to gain power. In education, these people might be teachers of subjects that have a smaller pool of qualified applicants, for example. Once people are hired to fill these roles, they may sense that there's a higher value placed on their roles and feel untouchable. If a coach who is an ineffective teacher or even an unpleasant person takes his team to state every year, his perceived value to the school may outweigh his lack of skill in the classroom—and he knows it. Some districts and states have even developed different pay scales for certain subjects. Although this may seem like a sensible solution to attract needed personnel, a pay disparity has the potential to significantly detract from the school culture.

When presented with a dilemma of this sort, it's important to remember that there are almost always other options. The leader should never feel so hamstrung that he or she cannot do what is right. The effort it takes to fill a challenging position should not diminish the importance of teachers in easier-to-fill positions. The factor of scarcity only underlines the importance of having an effective leader and a positive culture, so that quality teachers in *all* positions choose to stay.

Liking. *If I can go fishing with the principal, I bet he'll overlook those times when my students are out of control.* Do you see where this one is going? It pays to make friends with the boss. A weak teacher might join the principal in cheering the Chicago Cubs, playing golf, carpooling kids to soccer games, or anything else that might build a bond. Friendship makes it easy to deflect serious conversations about teaching effectiveness.

All teachers are aware that if they become too friendly with students, they may have a hard time assuming the role of disciplinarian. Teachers vary in where they draw this line, but they all know they cannot cross it if they want to be effective in the classroom. This is at least as true, if not more so, for principal-teacher relationships. There are certain teachers who are essential in helping the school move forward, but if they are perceived as the "principal's pets," their influence can quickly diminish. You can probably think of a veteran male principal who likes sports hanging around way too often with veteran male sports-loving teachers. If these teachers are outstanding, it may not become a problem, but if they're not, it can quickly hurt the principal's credibility and the faculty's morale.

There are several reasons why these five weapons work. First, we are human and thus susceptible to the manipulative effects of these tactics. Second, a toxic culture allows it. If a school has many weak longtime teachers, chances are that numerous people are playing these influence games. If the games are pervasive, they won't be seen for what they are. The culture will normalize these tactics, and the weak teachers will gain value and power that transcend their ability to teach well.

How *Not* to Change the Culture

So now we know how easily toxic cultures are formed and some factors that contribute to them staying that way. As you might imagine, it's no simple matter to turn such a culture around. We've seen many administrators bold enough to try to break out of these toxic narratives. In Chapters 3 and 4, we discuss how to do so effectively, but for now we will take a closer look at some less successful approaches that are commonly used by well-meaning leaders who are dedicated to building a better school culture—but that produce only short-lived change at best. In this section, we identify these approaches and explain why they are ineffective.

Letting personalities run roughshod over ideas and values. Personality-driven change is often tenuous. For example, a "champion" who represents the values and beliefs of the setting may seem to be the ideal figure to lead change—but what happens if the champion changes his or her mind about the initiative or leaves the school? Alternatively, personalities who have deep knowledge of the existing stubborn culture may secure a place for themselves by creating the mere illusion of making meaningful contributions to change efforts. Instead of letting personalities lead change, keep the focus on ideas and values, which are much more difficult to invalidate. Celebrate heroes and value colleagues, but don't depend on a personality to sell the future.

Using culture to sell a program. Beware of services or products that shoehorn in the concept of culture as a selling point. Presentations or publications that provide otherwise excellent ideas for school improvement may try to bring in the concept of culture as just another dependent variable that will be affected by these programs.

A promise or claim ending with "and culture" is a clue that culture is an aside or afterthought that was introduced to trigger more sales. It's people, not programs, that determine whether a culture changes for better or worse.

Failing to foster conversations across social groups. In all schools, people talk, even the introverts. Most adults have a group of people they prefer to hang out with. Often these groups create social boundaries, or informal silos (Louni & Subbalakshmi, 2014). In many schools, new ideas stay within the group they germinated from. Even if the principal brings new ideas to a meeting with all in attendance, the norm is to go back to one's PLC (personal lounge club) and debate the merits of the new ideas. If any attempts are made to deploy new ideas, teachers tend to share results within their groups; it would be rare for their results to affect other groups. Even when initiatives go well, teachers tend to celebrate within their individual social groups. This behavior, which is unfortunately the norm in many schools, nips in the bud the growth that could happen if the experiences were shared across groups. Teachers' lack of awareness of what other teachers are doing in the school is a red flag that the culture is not where it should be.

Rushing into culture overhauls and "kickoffs." As any national or state education conference draws to a close, many school leaders are eager to bring back and implement some new ideas. There is nothing wrong with this; excitement over new ideas is a good thing! But when each conference inspires a major new initiative accompanied by a big kickoff event that announces the arrival of a new culture, things aren't going to change. At best, the culture will find ways to make the celebration seem silly, and at worst, it will invalidate the whole effort. Changing culture requires informal conversations and a plan—not fanfare, signs, speeches, cake, or high-fives. Any time we use "stuff" to sell a new idea, we tend to forget about the stuff not being there in the future, leaving people with no reward motivating them to carry on with new behaviors. If the change is a great idea, it will sell itself.

Making a big investment of resources. Similar to the preceding issue, merely investing energy and resources into changing the culture will not work. We cannot buy people's values and beliefs. We need to ask them what is important and how we might protect those things. We need to ask what they are trying to protect when it seems their efforts are ineffective. Stipends, time off, new duties, or even a whole new school building will not drive people to see the world differently; those things will only provide a temporary climate change. The culture lives in people's minds and hearts. Sometimes it takes an investment in the whole community rather than individual success to motivate change (Bellah, Madsen, Sullivan, Swidler, & Tipton, 2007).

Assuming buy-in. The quickest way to end a meeting you do not enjoy is to agree with everything that is being asserted. Many people will gladly sacrifice their opinions of what matters if it gets them out of a dull or uncomfortable meeting. What is interesting is to see how many attendees will meet later in the hallway to discuss what was said and how they really feel. This "meeting after the meeting" is when people share their true values and beliefs—and vent about how annoying the meeting was and acknowledge that a quick adjournment was the real goal of the meeting. Just because everyone is smiling and nodding does not mean they have bought anything. Assuming buy-in at the level of cultural change will create a contrived school culture (Gruenert & Whitaker, 2015).

Promising happiness. If you as the leadership find yourself promising staffers a happy ending, you might be inadvertently pushing their "skeptic" buttons. Statistically, people are predictable; if you ask participants in an experiment to follow a specific set of instructions, the probability is high that the expected outcome will be achieved. But experiments are conducted in a controlled environment; education is anything but a controlled environment. If leaders need to promise something, promising that the culture will push back on any change and that some failures are inevitable is a fairly safe prediction. Happiness is not something that can be given or guaranteed.

Threatening doom. Issuing threats of a looming catastrophe may seem to be the opposite of promising happiness, but both these tactics use a possible external outcome to bribe or scare people into compliance. "If we don't do this, then the state will take over our schools, and many will lose their jobs." If that is the speech you give to introduce a change effort, good luck. If it takes a threat or a bribe to improve a school, it is because the culture has taught people that that is how things are done around here. Not to mention, compliance shouldn't even be the goal. Compliance does not lead to commitment; it kills it. Likewise, to manufacture a crisis and trick people into an urgent mindset does not change an existing culture; it challenges it. And the culture always wins.

Issuing new mandates to support a new culture. School leaders may try to let everyone know *they are there* by making a lot of noise or creating big footprints. New leaders might have some rooms painted or flowers planted, change the schedule, or create new rules in an effort to communicate that there is a new sheriff in town. A principal who has been at the school a long time may have been given a deadline by the new superintendent. Either way, we cannot mandate new values and beliefs. We cannot demand that teachers treat students in a positive manner and expect that demand to influence those who choose not to. New mandates are rarely followed either by those who struggle to follow rules *or* by those who have a record of success (why fix something that works?). New mandates that attempt to force behaviors tend to make the better teachers uncomfortable, which is a primary indicator that the mandate could make things worse.

Boasting a "culture of _____." Often, we hear school leaders professing that they will create a new school culture based on an honorable trait or value, such as caring, diversity, student achievement, or trust. To claim one has a culture *of* [insert value] is to declare that a particular culture possesses that trait. The problem is that all cultures likely have *some* degree of any value that could be named. Does a school that claims it has a culture of a given value just have a *stronger* degree of that value?

For example, if a leader stated that his school had a culture of caring, what would that mean? Even the worst schools have teachers who care about their students. Should we assume that in a school with a self-proclaimed culture of caring, caring serves as a major part of that school's identity? One would assume that in such a school, everyone cares about everyone, caring is an unwritten rule that new students and teachers learn quickly, and rituals and routines demonstrate to visitors that caring is a high priority in the school. A culture of caring implies that caring matters more than other organizational values that are not used to define the culture.

Another way of looking at it is to think of the culture of education in the United States. Within that culture, we might find a culture of teaching. Within the culture of teaching there might be a culture of teaching history. Within *that* culture might be a culture of teaching history in middle school . . . in rural regions . . . focusing on the Civil War . . . and so on. The process begins to lose meaning. At what point have we lost the power of culture as we try to groom it to fit a particular venue, trait, or need?

Our aim here is not to discredit people who claim they have a culture *of* something but, rather, to ask them to think about what they mean by it and how that claim, whether it exists in a mission statement or on a social media blurb, may cause confusion.

We did not develop this list of misguided approaches to shame anyone. School leaders who are trying to make positive culture changes have their hearts in the right place. Given the right circumstances, people can be manipulated or pressured into buying things that were never on their list or buying in to ideas that were never tested (Cialdini, 2018). Maybe a presentation or book has made changing the culture of a school seem easy, or the leadership needs a silver bullet, or a principal simply confuses climate with culture. And in times of compliance, urgency, and accountability, people will follow whomever talks about the easiest and quickest way to improvement.

These misguided efforts to effect sustained culture change can take administrators to any of a number of undesirable places. Read on for an example.

Using Misguided Approaches to Change the Culture: A Case Study

In this section, we delve into a scenario that illustrates what happened when a well-meaning principal used three misguided approaches—prioritizing personalities over ideas and values, assuming buy-in, and rushing into a culture overhaul—to attempt to change his school's culture.

When we were introduced to Mr. Johnson, he was starting his first year at the school and his first year as an elementary principal. The faculty had experienced many years of success, and student achievement was high. What made this high-performing school unusual is that, although the teachers were friendly with one another, they rarely worked together.

Mr. Johnson was anxious to bring in new ideas related to collaboration. His belief in working together was strong. He had worked on many team projects as a teacher, and his principal preparation program had reinforced the power of teams, PLCs, and teachers sharing and caring about their work in the classroom. He had spent time reading books about collaboration and attending professional conferences the summer before his first year of administrative duties. He wanted to introduce a whole new way of doing school, based on research, to take the faculty to better places.

He believed the first meeting in August with faculty was going to be a good one. According to our research (Gruenert & Whitaker, 2019), this meeting is the most powerful time to leverage new ideas into a school's culture. Mr. Johnson was stoked and assumed that everyone else would share his excitement and energy. The meeting got off to a good start, and when it was time to roll out his idea, he was well prepared with handouts, a PowerPoint presentation, activities, schedules, and forms. He was certain the faculty would celebrate the revival of a school stuck in the past, quickly adopt his ideas, and race toward improvement.

After Mr. Johnson had finished his presentation, he smiled and asked for volunteers to pilot a classroom exchange in which teachers would pair up to observe and provide feedback on each other's classes. He had anticipated that numerous staff members would be eager to be a part of this exciting initiative. At the very least, he assumed, the best teachers would readily join in, which would encourage others to follow their lead. Instead, the room filled with a stony silence—even the crickets stopped chirping—and none of the teachers made eye contact. Finally, after what must have seemed like an hour to everyone in the room, a single teacher hesitantly raised her hand to volunteer—possibly more out of a sense of duty than excitement—only to be greeted by subtle eye rolls and low-volume sneers from some of her colleagues. Because no one else raised a hand, the lone volunteer would have no partner to exchange observations with. Instead of being greeted as a risk-taking heroine, she felt like a social pariah. The discomfort in the room was palpable. After an awkward minute or so, Mr. Johnson moved on, feeling his confidence drain as a result of the lack of enthusiasm. He wasn't sure what to do next and decided to quickly wrap up the remaining items on his agenda.

The two most uncomfortable people in the room were Mr. Johnson and the volunteer. The most satisfied people were those who dreaded anything that was new or might require more work. After such a tepid response, it would be difficult to reintroduce this initiative, and Mr. Johnson felt like he'd lost points in a competition. The teachers' reaction to his ideas felt personal.

This was a good school with mostly caring teachers, so what happened? The principal introduced what seemed like a wonderful idea that would foster collaboration and tremendous professional growth. How could a group of successful professionals kill a great idea so quickly?

Mr. Johnson's biggest mistake was assuming that because the teachers were social outside work, and because he was armed with unassailable research and great tools to help them move forward, they would immediately embrace his new ideas as a team. As we know, though, assuming buy-in and rushing into culture overhaul are misguided approaches. His ideas were good, and he was correct that the potential for collaboration was there: if people choose to work alone but enjoy socializing away from work, you have an opening. But he had assumed logic was the answer, underestimating the invisible emotional undercurrent that intensifies when a culture feels threatened. One essential component of shifting a culture that Mr. Johnson had overlooked is not to force it. Few things get a culture to push back as much as attempts to effect change through perceived coercion.

Another mistake Mr. Johnson made was asking for volunteers with the entire culture watching. Even people who might have been eager to participate would have felt reluctant to come forward if they thought some of their more negative colleagues would steer their wrath in their direction.

If we have to ask people to collaborate, it may be because the culture has allowed them to experience success without collaborating. In the book *The Enemies of Leadership,* Bogue (1985) asserts that people who are able to lead effectively but choose not to are the real enemies of collaboration. At this school, the enemies of collaboration may have been the ones who collaborated often and effectively in *social* settings but chose not to in professional settings. Perhaps there were egos creating a pecking order, or maybe past experiences in group projects had not gone well.

It is difficult to ask people to collaborate when they have spent years and won awards without doing it. It is *very* difficult when there are people who simply do not like or trust one another. Many of the elements of this school's culture converged into strong beliefs that had been reinforced over time to define "how we do things around here." In this school, teachers valued autonomy and self-efficacy; collective efficacy was considered unnecessary. After all, evaluations were based on how each person performed, alone.

A Better Way

Now let's look at an alternative scenario in which our principal introduces the initiative more effectively.

First, Mr. Johnson lays the groundwork carefully. One thing he wants to accomplish this year is to get teachers into one another's classrooms. Knowing this is a primary goal, he had asked prospective teachers during their interviews what they thought about going into their peers' classrooms to observe and having peers in turn observe their classrooms, enabling everyone to share feedback and ideas. The interviewees, wanting the job, tended to respond positively. In this way, Mr. Johnson planted the seed that classroom visits would be a common practice at this school and got buy-in before the culture could tell the newcomers otherwise. These teachers started in the school assuming that teachers observe one another's classes in a nonjudgmental, nonevaluative way.

At the first faculty meeting in August, Mr. Johnson compliments the faculty on its success and says he is honored to be among such a dynamic group of talented educators. He mentions that one of his goals is to be in classrooms on a regular basis so that he can see all the wonderful things happening. He wants to learn how this school does so well.

Then, starting on day one, he goes into classrooms and asks individual teachers about the amazing things taking place in their rooms. Maybe they have a great questioning strategy, use longer wait times, set up an alternative seating arrangement, or even create a colorful bulletin board. He looks for the good in every room. He then leaves notes, sends complimentary e-mails, or just offers praise during a brief informal chat.

Mr. Johnson achieves several things with this simple practice. First, he is helping the teachers feel valued and therefore comfortable around him. Now, when someone comes into their rooms, they feel a sense of pride instead of feeling intruded upon. He is also learning what each teacher does best and identifying the most successful teachers in the school. This is key: know who represents the future, know who the best are, and be sure they know it. He can now find ways to let other teachers know where great things are happening and encourage them to go take a peek.

Next, Mr. Johnson targets the points of least resistance by engaging the best teachers and the new teachers. He has gone into the new teachers' classrooms starting on day one, so they feel comfortable having a visitor observing, and his positive feedback has boosted their confidence. Before long, he approaches one of the most effective teachers and asks her if a new teacher could come in and observe the specific thing she does best, whether that's working with reading groups, leading math activities, or getting class started in an engaging way. Because he is acknowledging that she is a skilled teacher, and because she will probably be more comfortable having a new teacher observe than a longtime colleague, she will likely agree. Mr.

Johnson makes sure to ask the veteran teacher to observe the new teacher's classroom in turn so that the activity is reciprocal rather than taking a "learn from the master" approach.

Assuming this goes well, Mr. Johnson approaches another effective teacher about doing a classroom observation swap. Gradually, he involves more and more staff members. Rather than blindsiding the faculty and bludgeoning the culture with a head-on assault and assumption that everyone will be on board, he is introducing the new idea in a way that's more comfortable and less threatening for the teachers, earning buy-in gradually and allowing a higher level of initial success. His idea has a better chance of going to scale when the better teachers begin to share its benefits.

He can anticipate some pushback from faculty members who have not been involved with the peer observation activities. The pushback may be subtle—perhaps a few jokes or cynical comments in informal gatherings. Mr. Johnson may not even know it is happening if the negative teachers choose to approach the new teachers, commenting about how they don't have time for this foolishness, or maybe inviting the new teachers to their classrooms to "see how real teaching happens." It could get ugly. The toxic teachers may broadcast that this new approach is not meant to make teachers better but to covertly evaluate them.

This is where Mr. Johnson can use what he has learned about school culture. He remembers hearing how people can shape a new culture and a new culture can shape people. He can also recruit the effective teachers who are engaged with the new teachers to help counteract the efforts of the negative teachers. He will need to let these chosen teachers know that the classroom observations may not sit well with other teachers. That conversation is critical, and ongoing. If there is no pushback, you may need to ramp up the effort a notch. This may seem counterintuitive, but pushback is often a sign that you have touched the culture. To do anything new and get no pushback—not even rolled eyes—means you haven't made any changes at the cultural level.

The negative teachers will use the past as evidence that they already know what they are doing. The effective teachers need to use the future. They need to have a vision, and then share that vision with others. Keep in mind that negative teachers collaborate, too. They tend to hang out together, share the same stories, prefer the same things, laugh at the same jokes. This is the illusion of a team that attracts unsuspecting teachers. This is a group of people who typically solve professional problems by complaining about how busy they are and that they already know how to teach. They can talk a good game because they have been doing it a long time. A principal who is aware of this dynamic will be better prepared to take the subtle first steps toward changing the culture.

When to Change the Culture— And When Not To

Up to this point, we've explored toxic school cultures that clearly need to be *recharged*. But sometimes it's tough to ascertain the extent to which a school culture needs changing. Not every issue a school faces indicates a need to change the culture; after all, even schools with healthy cultures have challenges. And sometimes change efforts can have the opposite of the intended effect. We have heard stories of principals who read our books and went completely bonkers with the stuff. Although we were initially happy to have made such an impression, as we continued to listen, we realized that a few teachers seemed worn out by all the new ideas and initiatives coming at them at such a fast pace. These school cultures are *over-charged*. So how can you tell whether your school culture is toxic, healthy, or overcharged?

The Supreme Court of the United States has delivered decisions on many cases that come with a "test" to determine whether the law has been broken, such as the Lemon test, which emerged from the case of Lemon v. Kurtzman and is applied to legislation concerning religion. In schools, we have found there are certain criteria that may be used to determine whether a change in the culture is necessary.

Let's start with the healthy cultures. The following are indicators of a truly collaborative school culture—in other words, signs that the culture is already healthy and efforts to change it may backfire:

- The discomfort of one brings discomfort to all.
- The mission of the school is compelling.
- The vision of the school is energizing.
- The notion of improvement spreads like a virus.
- The school is a place where people want to be.
- Staff feel professionally safe.

This list is a set of values or strengths that can leverage many new changes. This is not to say that a school with these qualities is perfect; that's an unreachable goal. The following issues may challenge schools' efforts to provide a safe, productive environment for students and teachers, but they do not in themselves warrant a change in the school's culture:

- A few parents are complaining about a teacher.
- A teacher is having a bad day.
- A few students are wearing hats inside the building.
- The football team is always losing.
- There's trash in the parking lot.

When leaders decide it is time to address the school culture, it should be because of deep-rooted issues that never seem to get fixed. Wanting your school's culture to mirror that of an amazing school you heard about at a conference last weekend or trying to prove your worth by shaking things up is not sufficient grounds for a culture overhaul. The following systemic issues are true indicators that school leaders need to take a closer look at their school cultures:

- There is a lack of trust among the adults.
- Unfriendly competition among teachers abounds.
- Support staff are taking sides.
- Teachers seem too busy to help their colleagues.
- Professional development is a joke.
- Policies are top-down, without teacher input.
- School improvement is an exercise in compliance.
- Motivation and morale have gone downhill.
- Teachers say, "These kids just don't care."
- Being negative feels good, and winning arguments over stakeholders is rewarding.
- Goals are constantly changing.
- The mission or vision is a source of jokes or sarcasm.
- The good people leave and the weak people stay.
- Whining works.
- Past failures are used as weapons (not just evidence).

Culture, for better or worse, makes certain behaviors so common you don't see them anymore. The culture will make each of the indicators in the preceding list seem normal if you let them hang around long enough. Instead of being recognized as toxic, these issues would bond the group and cement the culture.

It can be a challenge to know exactly when to start and how much of an initial push to make. Let's try an exercise. When you hear people talk about creating a collaborative school culture, which of the following do you suppose they mean?

- Scrapping the current culture and creating a new one
- Creating a second, additional culture
- Adding new values and beliefs to the current culture
- Requiring people to work together in PLCs
- Building structures to accommodate collaboration for the whole school
- Promoting new routines, rituals, and norms
- Sharing stories of collaborative successes
- Modeling collaboration as a leader
- Asking a few people to consider working together on some projects

After looking at this list, do you think some of these actions seem more laborious than others? Do some seem to require extra resources? Do some feel like too much, too soon? If we asked you to rank these actions from most effective to least effective, what would your list look like?

We believe the actions are already listed in order of effectiveness—with the items at the bottom of the list being most effective. Those listed at the top are not good strategies for any school leader who seeks to change the culture of his or her school, regardless of the situation. Trying to "become" a whole new culture is generally an exercise in futility. It takes less time to change a culture you already have than to create a whole new culture, and making incremental changes to what you've already got is certainly more realistic and less overwhelming.

In schools that rush to overhaul the culture with a flurry of new initiatives and ideas, the culture can easily become overcharged. In these schools, we may hear the following:

- "I wonder what type of culture we will have this week."
- "Just wait for this to blow over."
- "Can we wait until the dust settles for the next idea?"
- "My plate is full."
- "I am not sure who we are."

Here are some types of leaders who rush into culture overhauls, creating overcharged school cultures:

- *The legacy builder* is the leader who is nearing the end of his career and hopes to go out with a bang, perhaps with a statue of him out in front of the central office. To accomplish this, the leader needs to demonstrate how things have improved as a result of his efforts. To leave no room for doubt, this leader will bring many new ideas, people, structures, parties, celebrations, and testimonials to the faculty in an effort to buy their votes. Any of these events alone could be useful in a school improvement effort. When all of them hit the fan at the same time—well, there's a word for that.

- *The progressive* was hired because the board felt it was time for a change. They took a risk in hiring an individual who had some great ideas at the interview, though she didn't know what was actually feasible for this school because she isn't from around here. The first faculty meeting felt like a graduate course with handouts, lectures, new schedules, and new ideas accompanied by new forms and deadlines: PLCs creating tiered plans for all students, team teaching in all classes, the internet replacing textbooks, reflections captured in regular journal entries, a focus on the whole child with less concern about grading. By introducing all these initiatives, she's throwing everything at the wall to see what sticks. Instead of seeking out the best solution, she's looking for any solution to any problem. All of these can be great ideas to experiment with, but bringing them at full force, with little regard for tradition, just won't work in most settings.

- *The opportunist* shows up for a year or two, eager to build his résumé and use the position as a stepping-stone to a better one. For this plan to succeed, there needs to be a body of evidence that great changes have occurred while the leader was there. This is akin to the leader who is hired to clean house—which usually means to chase off anyone not in compliance. This might also be a person with a 10-page to-do list. Each month, or even week, will bring a new idea to try, with little regard for whether anything really made a difference. Success is defined as having brought new stuff to the school rather than as positive change. Perhaps the only thing that changed was the development of more subcultures ready to push back on the next idea.

We applaud leaders who strive for positive change and use the culture as a means for improving student outcomes and employee performance. We hope we have shed some light on when it might be too much, too soon, or when the motivation to change is misguided. If it ever seems like a culture changed quickly, remember: it didn't.

Summing Up

When a leader chooses to change a culture over the long term, his or her success comes down to commitment. Commitment, that quality inside each of us that unleashes our passion to improve, is the antidote to succumbing to fads, floundering amid complex personalities and other messy human factors, or giving in to panic in the face of competing demands. Once, we heard a person say, "If people had real passion, wouldn't they come to work for free?" That was the wrong question to ask. The better question is this: after winning the lottery, would you still come to work?

3

Building a
Trust-Based Culture

Many school improvement approaches are deficit-based: they react to the data with a strategic planning framework aimed at "fixing" the problem. They tend to be scripted, outlining step-by-step plans with deadlines for outcomes. The problem with this approach can be encapsulated in leadership guru Peter Drucker's famous statement that "culture eats strategy for breakfast." In other words, all the impressive strategies, plans, and frameworks in the world won't fix a school with a toxic culture. Instead, we recommend a trust-based improvement approach, which effects deep change by building relationships and a foundation of trust.

Because school culture, good or bad, takes root through the stories that are told in and about the school, the way we frame a school's narrative plays a major role in its culture. Accordingly, in this chapter, we explore the importance of stories in building positive, sustainable school cultures and focus on how to create change through trust, collaboration, and commitment rather than fear, competition, and compliance.

Tell Your Story

Part of understanding a school's culture is understanding how certain concepts have been defined, and events described, among the faculty. In a sense, nothing "happens" until a trusted person provides a narrative frame for it. For nearly every event that occurs in a school, there are internal stories shared among members of that school that tell what "really" happened and what it means. For example, at a faculty meeting, you can listen to a guest speaker talk about trauma-affected students who are struggling with academics. After this meeting, you might hear some teachers discussing students who they believe are experiencing these issues, see others walking away with the attitude that these darn kids just need to fall down once in a while, and observe still others feeling glad the meeting is over so they can get back to grading assignments.

Chances are the faculty members who are most respected will have their own versions. We call these *parking lot stories:* the meetings after the meetings, which also take place in the hallways and teacher workrooms. Leaders can let these conversations happen randomly and hope they support the mission and vision of the school, or they can get in front of the stories and provide their own master narrative that gives shape to what's happening. When leaders tell these stories, whether formally or informally, they bring meaning to what happened. If the leadership does not attend to this, the loudest people in the parking lot will.

Even the most boring or mundane meetings provide participants with something to talk about afterward. It's important for leaders to acknowledge when an event like a meeting or a professional development (PD) session was a boring disaster or failed to deliver good ideas. If a principal lets a bad meeting happen and chooses to do nothing, this ineffective meeting could be used as evidence by toxic teachers to discredit subsequent meetings or ideas presented by the principal. Toxic people love it when a bad meeting happens: they can bank it to oppose any future attempts at innovation.

A single event can yield various potential stories. Let's look at a faculty meeting where a few teachers have become emotional while describing their unproductive efforts with students and are reaching out to the group for help. As these teachers share how much they tried to make accommodations, create relevance, and experiment with differentiated instruction, some break down and cry.

In this emotionally charged meeting, what would the best teachers do? What would the negative teachers do? What would the toxic teachers do? All would see this meeting as an opportunity to leverage their own point of view, and each will leave the meeting feeling differently about what happened. The toxic teachers might gripe to one another about having to sit through an emotional session dominated by crybaby teachers, whereas more positive teachers might feel empathy toward their colleagues and offer to give them additional support. The leader can influence those impressions through her own actions. She could reinforce the notion of collaboration by providing time for a whole-group discussion, supporting the future collaboration of any teacher who is struggling. Or she could suggest that the struggling teachers meet together afterward and steer the meeting back to the agenda, treating the emotions as a distraction to what needs to get done. Whatever the leader does, it will provide the backstory for those who engage in future events with this leader. If the leader does nothing, she leaves this opportunity for growth to the discretion of whoever speaks the loudest after the meeting.

The stories being told today are what shape the future. If you choose to do nothing as a leader, the culture of the past wins, gets stronger, and makes this "do nothing" behavior seem normal so that people begin to trust that approach.

Build Trust

Many of us think improvement means targeting all the deficits that have been identified in our setting. How much do we let what's wrong determine what we do next instead of harnessing our strengths to build a stronger school? Is it possible to build a school improvement approach that uses trust instead of deficits as the primary framework? If culture eats strategy for breakfast, why feed it?

Instead of trying improvement strategies that may or may not work with the current culture, we recommend building a process that complements the way cultures are built and what cultures thrive on. Instead of using past failures to determine what to chase this year, use trust as the foundation for what happens next.

Figures 3.1 and 3.2 provide a visual of these two types of approaches. Figure 3.1 represents how schools with toxic, deficit-based cultures tend to do things, chasing the low numbers and using these numbers to scare people into compliance. Figure 3.2 presents a different approach that positive, trust-based cultures take; notice the similar flow, but with a few key differences.

Do you see where the stories fit in both figures? Each step is followed by a story, just as everyone who leaves a movie or a faculty meeting has his or her own idea of what happened. For example, some teachers may leave a PD session feeling threatened, as if what they are doing is substandard, whereas others may feel energized, feeling that they have been given permission to experiment with new approaches. Rarely will any two people have the exact same interpretation, although movie directors and school leaders alike hope these stories align with what they intend to be the takeaways from the experience.

FIGURE 3.1
Deficit-Based School Improvement: Reacting to Data with Strategies

FIGURE 3.2
Trust-Based School Improvement: Using Relationships to Build Trust

For the approach outlined in Figure 3.2 to succeed, the culture needs to be rich in *social capital*. The notion of social capital, which was introduced to the world in the early 20th century, speaks to the trust that is necessary for communities to thrive. In 1916, L. J. Hanifan defined it as the "fellowship, mutual sympathy and social intercourse among a group of individuals and families who make up a social unit" (p. 130). The trust among individuals in a community provides reasons to talk about the future rather than being stuck in the "good old days" of the past. Social capital is like insurance, almost a pre-forgiveness contract that allows for risk taking. When social capital exists inside schools, the issue of accountability becomes less of a mandate or threat to react to.

When we trust one another, we support one another. Just like when you and a partner spot each other bench-pressing, each of you pushes while also protecting the other. In the weight room, the idea is to work until failure occurs; we lift weights until we can't. Having a partner to get us to the workout, work with us as we get stronger, and be willing to fail (and watch us fail) without judgment is what trust-based improvement is all about.

Have you ever left a meeting feeling worse than you did when you went in? In some organizations, this is common: people drag their feet out of a draining meeting that has presented data focused on areas of deficiency or demanded improvement without offering support. By contrast, the flow of opportunities in trust-based school improvement energizes rather than demoralizes people, regardless of the content of the meeting. Each of the steps in Figure 3.2—learning, collaboration, efficacy, and commitment—provides a moment of success. Let's look at each step of the model:

- *Learning* is often seen as something only students do, but we purposefully use this word rather than *training*. Learning is more a change of mind than a change of behavior. The learning becomes real through collaboration.
- *Collaboration* is when teachers try to make sense of what they learned and allow the new learning to become useful. When we share our learning with others, we can also share how it fits in with our practice. When it works, it builds efficacy.
- *Efficacy* refers to the power to produce an effect, which powerfully boosts confidence. When we learn something new and put it into action and it works, our commitment to the process is elevated and we are open to the next new idea.
- *Commitment* is an intrinsic feeling that cannot be bought or bartered; it's when we achieve a high-enough level of belief in something that it builds a higher level of performance stability.

Again, the foundation of all these steps is trust. We need trust because we will make mistakes, and we need to be able to share them and learn from them. In unhealthy cultures, people may choose to hide mistakes that they perceive as embarrassing or damaging to their reputation. But a hidden mistake is easier to repeat than one that has been disclosed. And repeated mistakes become problems, problems become long-standing issues, and long-standing issues become the new normal. Get the picture?

Foster Collaboration

As we compare the models in Figures 3.1 and 3.2, we find that in the latter, learning replaces training, efficacy replaces apathy, and commitment replaces compliance. The change that will require the greatest effort, however, is moving from competition to collaboration. Collaboration strengthens that essential foundation of trust: trust is built when we listen to one another, which usually happens when we are sharing ideas, decision making, or problem solving—that is, collaborating. Leaders build trust when they listen to teachers, just as teachers build trust in the classroom when they listen to students.

For true collaboration to occur, the culture needs to value it. Learning, efficacy, and commitment all spring from collaboration— from our trusting one another as professionals. When a stubborn culture resists improvement, claiming that the school is fine as is and that any changes will make things worse, collaboration is how we convince the culture that what we choose to do next will be OK, even if it strays from tradition. Collaboration is the conversation that lets new ideas find purpose and builds collective efficacy to support a better future. When a group of people come together for a common purpose, things get done better and faster.

Collaboration is not a new concept. It has been dramatized in movies many times: think of the climactic scene in just about any sports movie where the coach declares that "we must come together as a team." Yet schools still lag in realizing the potential of collaboration.

One obstacle is the allure of the new. Education is particularly prone to embracing fads and bringing in new blood to shake things up. It can be difficult to see a different future if one has been at the same place for a long enough time, so many schools hire new leaders with the hope that these people will bring a fresh vision to a dreary place. The challenge comes when the new leader tries to force this new vision without paying any deference to what the teachers want. As Hanson (2009) observes, "you can push your own narrow agenda above all else, or you can redefine success as achieving bigger goals. . . . The Collaborative leader has the capacity to subordinate his or her own goals to the larger goals of the institution" (p. 151). The reality is, any changes that occur will be hybrids of the intended change. It's fruitless to try to completely transform a culture; there will always be pieces of the old one hanging on.

Let's look at a scenario from one school we worked with. Mr. Williams had finally gotten his dream job, becoming the principal of a school with a history of poor student achievement. That's right, he *wanted* to lead a low-performing school. While most of his professional experiences had been at high-achieving schools, his administrative preparation had lit a fire in him to make a difference at a school that needed *him*. He signed the contract in June, and school started in August. He had the better part of three months to set many pieces into motion. He met with the superintendent throughout the summer to affirm his intentions and to instill more confidence in his capacity to make changes in central office personnel. As the beginning of the school year neared, his changes became more obvious.

The word got out among the faculty and staff that there was a new sheriff in town making big changes. Mr. Williams had removed a few assistant coaches in the fall sports programs and hired some academic coaches, changed the academic schedules for many teachers to accommodate coteaching opportunities, and had the exterior of the building painted and landscaping added. He even rearranged the furniture in the main office. Most of these changes, made in the name of improvement, came as a surprise to the employees of that school. He was on a mission, it seemed, by himself. To others, he seemed to have a narrow agenda. The dominant parking lot story was that his goal was to establish a legacy at a poor school to help him ascend career-wise; not many believed he actually intended to go the distance. As a result, their strategy was to wait him out, resisting his efforts as much as possible.

Mr. William's intentions were good, but his method was to strong-arm. Often, we see "go-getters" like him attempt to bring major changes to a school in short order. They seem impervious to suggestion while they forge their new vision. But even if all these changes are great ideas, the culture demands a level of trust before any of it will have a chance of working. Even if the school board wants the new principal to "shake things up," without trust and collaboration, the principal at best will gain compliance with deadlines, not commitment to a new vision.

Mr. Williams gradually became more aware of the current culture during his first year at the school. As he visited with teachers, he began to understand the pace at which the school could change, and whom he could use to sell that change. Some of his ideas changed in structure, although not in essence. He managed to convince the superintendent that, although some of his promised changes may not happen quickly, he was confident in whom he was working with. His second year felt more like a team effort.

One of his goals was to create interdisciplinary teams, with the intention of both enhancing curriculum development and encouraging teachers to build stronger relationships with one another. The initial reception was mixed: some teachers were excited about joining these teams, and some did not want others encroaching on their territory—their subject matter and teaching approaches. Mr. Williams reasoned that if he could get a few teachers to experience success with this team approach, others would want to try it. For the first team, he deliberately recruited the best teachers, stacking the deck.

Over time, the team experienced many successes (as well as a few disappointments), and others became curious about the initiative and wanted to build their own teams. Mr. Williams had not anticipated the initiative expanding so quickly, so he controlled the pace by setting some limitations. First, he was clear about the purpose of the project to discourage the development of social groups. He also asked interested teachers to first visit with the pilot team and observe the team members conducting meetings and teaching before coming to him with a proposed team. He also explained that he would have the last call on who would be in what team. Setting these guidelines gave the initial team time to work out any bugs and prevented ineffective teams from developing and killing the project.

Rather than suddenly declaring the school a PLC zone, Mr. Williams led with a light hand and let the first team develop at its own pace, giving others in the school time to get used to the idea, to witness its success, and to feel excited about joining a team of their own. It took about three years before the idea of interdisciplinary teams was no longer a new thing. It was now part of the culture and served as a leading lever for culture change.

Gain Deep Commitment

In the preceding scenario, we touched briefly on compliance versus commitment. True culture change requires deep commitment.

Unlike compliance, commitment is not driven by deadlines or gained through threats or bribes. Commitment means leaders are making a long-term investment in people (Hanson, 2009): not only do leaders get the best out of their staff members, but staff members in turn also expect leaders to give their best. There is no quick road to commitment. Externally imposed changes can trigger the road to commitment, but too much, too soon, or a lack of relevance will push back even the strongest teachers as they try to just get through a day of work.

We believe commitment exists on a continuum, from superficial to all-out passionate. This is something easy to see in the weight room: some people are clearly there to socialize, some are there to work out, and some are there to test their limits. This can also become obvious at meetings where people are asked to identify their core values. What typically happens is that a few will share aspirational values: the things they wish they did rather than the things they currently do. If you are truly passionate about something, others should see it—that is, people should be able to tell what you're most passionate about by observing you. If collaboration is an organizational value, people should be openly collaborating most of the time, in most places. We can clearly call B.S. at meetings where people brag about valuing diversity when there is clearly little diversity present. An organization is dysfunctional when its people are not able to dedicate time and energy to what they believe is most important; it is a recipe for burnout.

Commitment is what we use when we try to stop smoking, lose weight, or learn a new language. We may have developed old habits that once defined who we were but now make change very difficult.

One of the most challenging leadership situations is to attempt to improve a school where you have been the leader for many years. There will be several rituals and routines that are embedded in the school's daily practices that obstruct change, just as people who are trying to change their exercise and eating habits will find reasons to justify missing a few workouts or grabbing a Twinkie. A good way to get teachers to own any new idea is to show how it makes a difference. After all, teachers become teachers to make a difference in students' lives. If the leader can demonstrate how helpful a change or an initiative is, commitment will follow.

Only with deep commitment can the members of a school community engage in continuous improvement. Continuous improvement is crucial to shifting the culture, but try not to let the concept become a stressor: the enemy of continuous improvement is perfection. Note, too, that continuous *improvement* does not mean continuous *culture change*. A quick culture change is a contradiction in terms, and any aim to achieve it is an attempt to avoid the necessary discomfort associated with the transformation of beliefs. Sudden positive behavior changes are often welcomed by organizational leaders and temporarily improve the climate—at least until the stimulus to change goes away. But anthropologists know that a culture does not change simply because a few people have chosen to behave differently. The new behaviors are simply compliance to external stimuli and rarely signal a permanent or long-term change. Compliance short-circuits commitment; it will never get the best efforts from employees. And if compliance hangs around too long, "good" becomes "good enough," and commitment silently atrophies.

Shift the Narrative

Let's revisit the significance of narratives. Imagine your favorite football team won a game by the score of 14 to 7. Depending on your own narrative about the team, you may be upset that the score was that close, or you may be happy the team actually won a game. Now imagine a 3rd grade teacher resigning in the middle of the school year. Would the dominant reaction be "We know she was having personal issues; we wish her the best," or "There goes another one jumping from a sinking ship"? If your school scored a few points higher this year than it did last year on the annual state test, would teachers say, "Those students put out a strong effort this year!" or "Seriously? We only improved by a few points, after all that extra work?"

As we have discussed, a big part of leaders' role is relaying the narrative that frames how people should think of or react to each important event at a school. The challenge is that sometimes the stories that permeate the school have a negative tone or are being told by people who do not have leadership roles.

Often, we find that those who speak for the school in various forums are those who have been there the longest. This isn't necessarily a bad thing; in schools with positive cultures, these folks will usually present information with a sense of pride, telling stories that accentuate past successes and paint positive images of past and present faculty. These positive stories help build the foundation for a positive future.

In some schools, though, the stories are not positive. In these schools, the people who speak the most tend to share stories of failures and ongoing issues that plague the school. It is almost as if they expect something good to come from sharing the bad. We want to ask these people, "What are you trying to protect?" When these stories dominate the conversations in the hallways, in faculty meetings, and even in the grocery store with parents, people will begin to believe they are true. If the leadership does nothing, the culture will allow these negative topics to define the school. When this becomes the status quo, the leader needs to step up and shift the narrative— that is, replace the negative stories with positive stories. Let's look at a principal who did just that.

After many weeks of grueling interviews and travel, Mrs. Jones finally landed the job she had always wanted: a middle school principal position in her hometown. During the last 20 years, she had gone to college, earned her teaching degree, taught in three different middle schools, gotten an administrative license, and served as an assistant principal, all in different states. As she reflects on the hiring process, she thinks it was her answer to a difficult interview question that made the difference. When asked, "What will you do during your first year as principal here?" she said that she would listen to the stories being told and try to change the ones that did not reflect well on the school.

Listen to the stories being told. In any school, these stories abound and are told by teachers, support staff, parents, and community members. Some stories will be true, and some may have bits of truth. Some will just be silly stories. Some will have influenced most people's perceptions of what kind of school this is. Mrs. Jones's challenge was to catalog these stories and determine which ones were not healthy for the school—which stories might scare away strong teachers from applying here or glorify an ineffective behavior or person. Being a hometown person, Mrs. Jones may have already known these stories, and she may have had some of her own, as she attempted to rebuild a questionable past. Stories of success from the past and stories that reveal an exciting future were necessary if the school was to improve.

During her first year, Mrs. Jones was able to downgrade the negative stories, even the ones that had some truth to them, and amplify the more positive stories she heard. She went to the places where the stories were told—in the hallways, lunchroom, parking lots, and after-school events. Whenever she heard people saying bad things about the school or bringing up a negative event from the past that seemed to have shaped the present, her response would try to defuse the negativity of the story and stop its trajectory—for example, by sharing something positive that ultimately emerged from the event.

One such story centered on the time a school board member who was good friends with the basketball coach threatened the principal after the principal declared that the best player on the basketball team couldn't play in the upcoming game owing to disciplinary issues. In this small town, the story spread like wildfire. Although the events had transpired 30 years ago, the story came up every time the current principal tried to apply disciplinary measures to any basketball player. Apparently, the board member and the coach had gotten their way, and since then, coaches had been granted outsize levels of power.

Mrs. Jones heard this story as some parents were waiting for their children to finish basketball practice. The new season—a highlight for this town—was about to begin. Sitting in the bleachers watching the coach run his players through some final drills, she thought this would be a good opportunity to change a narrative. She leaned over to the parents and said, smiling, "This coach would never put the school in such an awkward position." The next morning, she met with the coach to be sure they were on the same page. She related the story from the past as well as her response to the parents, shared her love of sports and how much pride students felt playing on the school's teams, and concluded by saying how much she enjoyed watching the coach work with the players and that she would be one of the team's strongest supporters.

Throughout the season, she made sure to meet with teachers in the hallways between classes just to socialize. She would sometimes bring up the 30-year-old story, exclaiming that she could not believe it had actually happened, and ask the veteran teachers how much of it was true. During these conversations, she would find a way to affirm that things had changed, and that the school was not the same school it had been in the past. This became the new story. It also let everyone know that athletes did not have immunity from discipline. There was no doubt in Mrs. Jones's mind that this story was being shared throughout the school, along with a few others she had told.

Keep in mind that these new stories need to be strategically placed and shared with regularity. Returning to Figures 3.1 and 3.2, we see those pivotal moments when leaders tell their stories, for better or worse. When leaders shift the narrative in a positive way, these stories become a constant drumbeat that drowns out the negative noise with hope.

Commit to a New Vision

With any change, there will be implementation dips as well as improvement spikes—which means there will be times when everything seems great, and times when things are not so great. A strong vision will get you through the challenging times. As Potter and Hastings (2004) put it, "Leaders with vision assume anything is possible. Without vision, we can see a difficulty in every opportunity. As we develop vision, we see an opportunity in every difficulty" (p. 79). If an organization wants to experience positive change, its vision will need to be stronger than its mission. We cannot let who we are and why we are here—that is, our mission—set limits on who we could be.

One elementary school principal we worked with was able to build a new vision with the faculty simply by asking them where they wanted to be in five years. Dr. Wilson was in his third year as principal at this school. During the first two years, he had spent time listening to faculty and support staff, counseling out some of the employees who needed to retire or move on, and establishing trust with as many people in the school and community as possible. Early in his third year, he walked up to a few teachers standing in the hallway and asked, "What do you hope will be different around here in five years?" After giving a few silly responses, which was typical of this group (and a necessary trait of educators), they got serious. Their responses surprised Dr. Wilson, because they didn't have any ideas.

Leaders do not need to wait until their third year at a school to start these conversations, but it helps if they have built a reserve of trust, which yields more sincere responses. Dr. Wilson asked these teachers to think about it and share their ideas later on—no deadlines, no expectations. But he knew he had asked the right people when, two days later, they came to him bringing a list and a sense of excitement. He also knew that positive people attract positive people. Now he had a handful of new potential directions the school could go in, without having had to devote much time or energy trying to convince teachers that they were good ideas: his small group of newly excited teachers did that for him.

Leaders should not ask "Who would teachers listen to?" but, rather, "Who *are* they listening to?" When we ask teachers where they hope to go in the future, we are not critiquing what they have been doing; we are giving them permission to dream. Dr. Wilson presented the teachers' ideas to the larger faculty and sustained conversations around them in the hallways, lunchroom, and parking lot. As time passed, other teachers began approaching Dr. Wilson with ideas. He did not take every idea to a faculty meeting for a vote, but decided to bring the three ideas that had seemed to resonate most strongly throughout the building. From that point on, the conversations were more about ways to support the ideas than debates on the merits of the ideas themselves.

One idea that garnered strong support was the development of a student curriculum committee. Yes, they were going to ask elementary students to help build and refine the curriculum. Students interested in being on this committee were asked to interview, sharing their strengths and visions for potential changes in how the school did education. The meetings were held after school, with supper provided, and one teacher from each grade level also sat on the committee. Committee members developed norms of collaboration; did "homework," which usually meant taking polls of other students or community members; made presentations to the principal and the school board; and celebrated successes.

Serving on the committee was a two-year position, and when someone left, it was exciting to watch students prepare to interview for the spot. The stories that emerged from these meetings glorified student participation, empowered student voices, and made the school a fun and relevant place to be. This committee was not treated as something just for show; faculty wanted it to be meaningful to the students. The idea became a new refrain heard throughout the school, proclaiming, *Students matter*.

Summing Up

One of the points we cannot emphasize enough is this: *you can do anything once you stop trying to do everything*. Slow and purposeful is as fast as leaders should go when aiming to shift the culture. Whereas getting people to behave differently in the short term is transactional leadership, true culture change requires transformational leadership.

Navigating lasting culture change is about providing meaning and weaving emotional threads throughout the setting. Culture is in our minds, right next to the emotional places we draw comfort from. Culture gets into our minds through the telling of stories, the stories we believe. Want to change the culture? Change your mind. Change the stories.

4

Sustaining Culture Change

So far, we've asked some big questions about the nature of culture, examined toxic school cultures, and looked at how to build trust-based cultures. The stark contrast between the toxic and positive cultures we've explored highlights where poor decisions led some astray and where laying a strong foundation for change led others toward success. Examining the differences in these approaches gives us some notion of where to concentrate our efforts to shift the cultures at our own schools.

In our work, we've come to know that just one book or presentation can ignite educators' curiosity about the culture of their school, driving them to reflect on the type of culture they work in and the type of culture they desire. To actually take steps to change the culture in a sustained way, however, takes much more commitment and focus than many realize. Accordingly, in this chapter, we offer advice on how to maintain your focus and avoid distractions as you tackle the difficult task of sustained culture change. In particular, we explain how to reduce toxic teachers' influence, get to know two additional prominent actors in the culture, engage in culture change thoughtfully rather than fashionably, and avoid culture change that is too rapid.

Reduce Toxic Teachers' Influence

Because cultures are made up of people, leaders must become intimately acquainted with the social networks in their buildings and engage strategically with both positive and toxic "actors" to diminish toxic teachers' influence.

We don't hire toxic teachers; we let new teachers join the wrong gang. Here's one way this can happen: a new teacher finds an aspect of the organization that seems confusing or dysfunctional and, rather than approaching leadership with the concern, he or she brings it to another faculty member. If that faculty member is a negative or toxic person, he or she will likely offer a negative or cynical response that makes apparent sense; it will probably have history and tradition supporting it. But any response by a toxic teacher regarding a frustrating issue will support future toxic behaviors.

Toxic teachers cannot thrive alone. Their strength relies on the support of others who sympathize with them, which means they are constantly recruiting. If you can drain the toxic club of its members, you can rid the school of toxic sentiments held by any teacher. Making sure the numbers in a toxic group never increase is an essential first step to turning the culture around. Once you stop the influx of membership in a toxic subculture, you can work to dismantle the group by reducing its reach and influence.

This approach also enables you to work with negative teachers who are not as far gone as the toxic teachers. Negative teachers not only are easier to bring over to the positive side than toxic teachers but also make great recruiters of those still stuck in toxicity. We recommend the following approaches to lessen the influence of toxic teachers.

Protect new teachers. Because the most vulnerable figures in a toxic school culture are new staff members, we recommend proactively ensuring that they don't connect with teachers who are the gateway to negativity or toxicity—or at the very least make it as difficult as possible for them to gain access to their less positive colleagues.

Leaders can do this simply by being thoughtful and deliberate about assignments and structures. For example, be intentional about assigning mentors to new teachers; don't leave it up to "convenience factors" such as grade level, location, gender, age, or planning time. Make these decisions based on whom you want new staff members to emulate or influence. The same thought process should go into assigning classrooms, planning time, lunch cycles, and so on.

To go even further, apply this same thinking to all staff members to try to curtail growth of toxic subgroups. Toxic teachers who have strong or intimidating personalities should be connected only with staff members whom they cannot sway. Cliques and subgroups are often formed on the basis of factors like room location and planning time. By thinking through these connections carefully, you will be able to limit toxic club membership.

Give the less committed toxic teachers a reason to leave the group. Rather than trying to dismantle a toxic group wholesale, it is often more productive to start with the less committed members. This tactic may have our instincts screaming—*we want to take down the leaders!*—but the leaders are often more dug into toxicity than the other group members. Some members of a toxic group may have just fallen in with the wrong crowd and can be extricated without too much difficulty. Most people would much rather enjoy work than not, after all. And we know that when we surround ourselves with gripers, it is very easy to find ourselves behaving in a similar manner.

If a school has a group of five teachers who gather in the teachers' lounge every morning to gripe and whine, we may assume that all five members are similar. However, any group is typically composed of leaders and followers. And the followers in a toxic group are usually fragile and weak people who just want to fit in somewhere. Members of these groups will even gripe about one of their own, if that person is absent that day—and everyone in the group knows it. Imagine wanting to fit in so badly that you are willing to hang around people who you know put you down when you are not around. If the leader can provide ways for these people to connect with more positive groups, they may jump at the chance.

After you have identified the people in your school who seem to be keeping the toxic behaviors alive, determine which are the least committed members of that subculture and draw them away. One of the most effective yet simplest ways to do this is to invite your best teachers to engage with the weaker subculture members. This can be formal, through deliberate development of certain committees, PLCs, planning times, extra duties, and mentoring partnerships. It can also be informal, by asking a strong, positive teacher to seek out a certain weak teacher in the hallways, join him or her during lunch, or sit close by during faculty meetings. This is a nonconfrontational approach that uses organizational culture as the tool to attempt to reorganize the social network of a few teachers. Should these targeted teachers be new teachers, this should serve as a warning that the current system of new teacher induction is not working.

Remember that there is no such thing as a toxic leader without toxic followers. Diminishing the number of followers who support these leaders—or even just feign support to avoid leaders' wrath—will significantly weaken the power of these central figures. If they have no one remaining in their camp, they may have to change their ways and relocate to a less toxic setting to avoid being alone. And if they do not change and just become more isolated, that may in itself be beneficial.

Disengage from toxic leaders. The culture of any school will not be completely supportive of any changes, even positive ones, until the story about the dominant yet ineffective teachers changes. Once toxic teachers are no longer heroes, the story can begin to change.

A nonconfrontational approach we recommend involves purposefully not engaging in toxic circular talk with those who, out of self-interest, want the future to look like the past. Making great teachers feel good is easy. The challenge comes when the veteran teachers who have not been invited to help build the future realize they have been shut out. They may choose to put up a fight, spreading gossip or maligning the change efforts to others; anticipate this, refuse to fan the flames, and know that your change efforts will cause some division. This period of discomfort is a necessary phase as you grow toward a more positive culture.

Support and increase the effectiveness of staff members. When teachers feel supported, they have less of a desire to be a part of negativity or toxicity. The converse is true, too: teachers who don't feel supported are much more susceptible to toxic influence. For example, imagine a new teacher feeling stressed about making his first "negative" phone call to a parent. If the principal role-plays making the call with the teacher, invites the teacher to listen in on one of her own challenging calls, or even offers to sit next to the teacher when he initiates his first couple of difficult calls, the teacher will feel less vulnerable and better set up for success.

If instead, as often happens, the principal leaves the new teacher to make his first difficult phone call on his own and it does not go well, that new teacher will get rattled emotionally. He may feel desperate for support and go into the teachers' lounge to describe what happened. If the strongest personality in that room is a toxic person, that negative colleague may knowingly say, "That's why we don't call parents around here." The new teacher's vulnerability and need for an emotional mentor provide an opening for the toxic colleague to become that teacher's strongest support and go-to person in times of distress.

When a school fails to consistently provide staff members with skills and supports, it works against itself, opening up opportunities for negativity to flourish and boosting the power and influence of toxic players. Sometimes people we think are insubordinate are actually ineffective in some area and just feeling frustrated. One of the biggest areas to look at is classroom management. Everyone wants to be a skilled classroom manager, so when teachers struggle in this area, it is often because they do not know a better way. If we do not help them become competent, they are much more likely to join the "kids nowadays" club and fixate on student misbehavior rather than focusing on the behavior that they can most easily influence: their own. As we build teachers' skills and confidence, we will naturally hear less complaining. The reason the very best teachers seem to gripe less about student behavior is because students behave better in their classrooms.

It's also essential to make sure that people feel valued. When we demonstrate that we value staff members, they are less likely to seek out validation from negative or toxic colleagues. Leaders, whether formally or informally, can intentionally look for ways to boost the self-worth of teachers. This can be even more crucial during the times of year when there are long stretches with no breaks. We all know influencing culture is not an event, but there are times when it is especially important to remind teachers what a difference they are making in the lives of students.

Diminishing Toxic Influence: A Case Study

Remember Ms. Garcia, the principal from Chapter 1 who wanted teachers to watch and learn from one another in a non-evaluative way? To achieve this goal, she had two jobs to do: (1) build a team of effective teachers to help produce a new movie with no room for toxic actors, and (2) protect teachers from adopting toxic roles in her school's movie and from being influenced by toxic colleagues. The best teachers in the building had been waiting for someone to change the plot and welcomed the opportunity to write new scripts that would improve the school. Ms. Garcia met informally with her new teachers to assure them that they were the future of the school and invite them to envision what that future might look like. She also privately let her best teachers know that they were her standard bearers and asked if they would like to work with a few new teachers to help design a new vision. Instead of prioritizing fitting new teachers into the current culture, this vision would incorporate the new teachers' voices, hopes, and dreams and capitalize on their enthusiasm for teaching, giving the initiative an extra boost. It was not long before the new teachers were hanging out with the best teachers. This is professional development at its best.

For her second task, Ms. Garcia recognized that it was her job to protect teachers during this fragile transition, when they were taking risks and making themselves vulnerable; it was not the teachers' job to stand up to their negative colleagues. If someone had to draw the ire of the few really toxic individuals, it should be the principal.

With previous principals, the toxic teachers had enjoyed a disproportionate level of influence, and Ms. Garcia did not want to grant them that same power during the change effort. She realized that when she gave them the floor to vent, it caused everyone else in the room—the positive and caring majority—to tense up and feel frustrated or self-conscious. So, during conversations about the future, Ms. Garcia began simply ignoring cynical or mean-spirited input and obvious attempts to snuff out positive change. She never did so in a cutting or cruel fashion; she would just smile and nod and change the subject or move on in a professional way. Sometimes she said she would love to meet privately with the teachers to hear more about their ideas and develop a better understanding of their views. She only ignored the contributions of the most hard-core toxic staff—those few who continually attacked any positive person or idea.

Ms. Garcia's strategy to ignore snide comments, negative sighs, and other unprofessional reactions was very frustrating to the cynics in the building. The more they tried to sabotage Ms. Garcia and her plan, the wider the gulf grew between them and other faculty members. The average teachers began to sense that a better future was coming that didn't include these few lazy, ineffective teachers. Even some of the negative teachers were waking up and recommitting to be the teachers they had aimed to be when they were hired. The toxic teachers persisted in their ways, but gradually their numbers and influence dwindled. Other teachers felt empowered by Ms. Garcia's approach to negativity and began to follow suit. With toxic people no longer getting the attention they craved, their only path to achieve recognition was to join the increasing numbers working to improve the school.

Regardless of how many toxic, negative, and positive staff members are in a school, the most important thing to focus on is which way these groups are trending. If you start with 10 toxic staff members and winnow that group down to 7, the group knows that it is weaker and more exposed. Conversely, as the strongest positive staff members connect with one another and join forces with new teachers each fall, the positive group increases in size and confidence.

Ms. Garcia's initiative did not require extra resources, formal announcements, or new policies or mandates. All it took was her using the current structure of the culture as a means for resolving a nagging issue. As a culture grows more positive, it also grows stronger. Eventually, word will get around that this is a good school to work at. Teachers committed to doing the right things will show up, and the toxic teachers who cannot or will not change will leave.

Engage the Other Actors: The Guardians of the Past and the Outliers

Up to this point, we've focused on the toxic actors in the school culture movie. But there are two other types of actors that can present challenges and have a strong influence, too. The leader's job is to understand their point of view, harness their strengths, and recruit them to be part of the culture change.

Finding Common Ground with the Guardians of the Past

What about those actors who share our values but hold us back? Guardians of the past—those who guard the future by using the past to make decisions—have more in common with us than we might initially think. To discover our common ground, though, we have to find the guardians, understand them, and recruit them as a powerful voice in our change efforts. A glance of approval from a respected guardian can command as much motivation as a paid speaker—and a look of disapproval can demotivate colleagues just as easily. We need to use the current culture to sell the next one. Rather than trashing the past, we can use it to our benefit.

We cannot completely ignore the warnings of our respected veteran staff when they claim something won't work at the school. The first step is to listen to the voice of the culture in your school. Ask teachers why they are at the school. Then ask them what they are trying to protect at their school. Chances are that most will share statements from the past that have echoed through the halls for generations. For example, in many schools, the veteran teachers have long lived under the threat that they must raise test scores or bad things will happen. So when someone proposes an initiative designed to foster students' social-emotional skills, the experienced teachers in the back of the room may roll their eyes and whisper to one another, "Don't they know it's all about test scores around here?" Even if the status quo isn't making them feel fulfilled, there will be a sense of "protecting" something. This is what we call the guardian voice. Try discussing any of the following topics to see how the guardians respond:

- What is the purpose of education?
- How does one get promoted around here?
- What does great teaching look like in this building?
- Why do students drop out of our schools?
- As educators, what should we guard against?

After you have listened to the guardians and understood where they're coming from, ask these important follow-up questions:

- When should we listen to our inner guardian of the past, and when should we override it?
- When is the past relevant, and when is it holding us back?

Even more pointedly, you can ask this multiple-choice question to see where teachers' priorities lie:

> When we are tasked with improving the school and are not sure what to do next, we decide our course of action based on
>
> (a) What is good for the kids.
>
> (b) What supports our survival.
>
> (c) What will raise test scores.
>
> (d) What will appease the administration.

These questions and the ensuing discussion should open up the eyes of the faculty to see that the past is not always the answer to current challenges. Once you have listened to and expressed respect for the guardians' point of view, they should be more amenable to opening up their own thinking to new possibilities.

The folks trying to guard the school's culture are not spiteful saboteurs; they are taking lessons from the past, perhaps selectively, and applying them to the future. *Stability* is their watchword. They may not choose (a) all the time, but we should not shame our guardians for trying to protect the school. They need to know we are all committed to the same thing and that taking some risks for the sake of positive change can be a good thing.

Valuing the Outliers

Once we can better manage our interactions with the actors who are reluctant to take new paths toward sustained culture change, it's time to turn to those actors who can help propel us forward.

Enter the outliers. Most organizations have at least one person who continually plays devil's advocate or whose ideas seem to stem from having had too much fun in the 1970s. Believe it or not, these people might well have something of value to contribute to school culture change.

Sometimes it seems as though search committees' primary criterion is just to find people who "fit in." Given this scenario, it is no wonder change happens at a glacial pace. It's natural, in a way: you want new people to fit in, and new people likewise want to fit in. But new ideas usually come from people who do not look like us or think like us. Unfortunately, in our world, that gives them two strikes before they ever get a chance to challenge the status quo.

However, once in a while, a teacher who does not fit in stays anyway. Can you think of anyone like this in your school? The teachers whom the culture has deemed the "weirdos"? If not, maybe your school needs a pain-in-the-rear person to get a few new ideas on the drawing board. You may already have some of these outliers who have great ideas but hesitate to offer them, fearing risk to their membership status. Maybe some have learned to remain silent from past experiences of offering an idea only to be shot down.

The response a person gives to a situation can either fit a norm or give that person (temporary) outlier status (see Figure 4.1). For example, if, during a heated conversation about last night's baseball game you say something positive about the St. Louis Cardinals, you

FIGURE 4.1
How a Culture Gains Strength

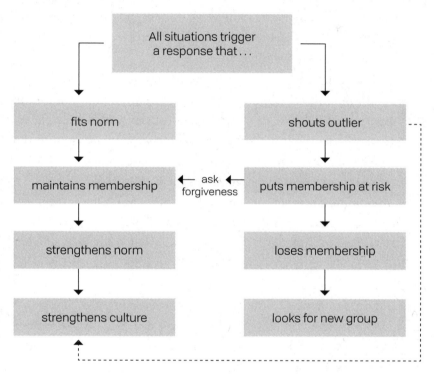

A culture gains strength both when members fit in and are rewarded accordingly *and* when outliers go against the grain and are punished accordingly.

have fit into the norm of that group. If you instead decide to say, "Who cares? It's just a game," you will probably get some quizzical or even hostile looks from the others. It's no big deal to disagree with people, but if almost everyone follows the Cardinals and you make a comment that actively goes against that norm, you have created some distance. The others will let you know that you stepped outside the norm and that your membership in the group has taken a small hit. Your next move, if you don't want to remain an outlier, is to make amends in some way—for example, by backtracking ("Just kidding!") or saying something apologetic or self-deprecating ("Yeah, I know, I'm weird!").

Either way you go will strengthen the culture. If you choose to fit in, you will validate the norm and the culture will thank you for the support. If you choose to violate the norm, you will be challenged. Attempting to repair the rift or correcting your course back to the norm strengthens the culture. Losing membership in the group after too many violations strengthens the culture, too.

Spending too much time in outlier status can cost you membership in that culture—unless you find a way to short-circuit the flow. Let's return to Figure 4.1. The dashed line denotes how a violation of a norm—a temporary jump into outlier status—can actually make the culture stronger. That is, a person who does not fit in can help build the future while simultaneously strengthening the culture.

What might this "jump" actually look like in an organization? Some people in your school likely have some outlandish ideas about how it may become more effective. Is it possible that an outlier might be the best resource for dreaming about the future? Is it possible to shape a culture that encourages outlier thinking? How could there ever be a convergence of values and beliefs if there is always a call to think outside the box—that is, the culture?

We've established that everything that happens in school strengthens the culture. When people follow the rules, they are rewarded; when they don't, they are punished. Both these results strengthen the current culture because they both fit expectations. Therefore, one way to weaken a culture—that is, to make it vulnerable to positive change—would be to reward those who break the rules. How's that for crazy thinking?

How do you think the guardians in your school would react if you praised the work of someone who's known for being a little weird? Imagine a social studies teacher in a PLC meeting relating how she had recently decided to scrap her lesson plan 20 minutes before class and sketched out a few new ideas on a napkin. Instead of coming in with a detailed lesson plan and a stack of worksheets, she led a conversation with her students about a current event that seemed to replicate an event from 200 years ago. The impromptu lesson went so well that she dared others to change everything 20 minutes before class—not all the time, but as an occasional way to stir up the teaching fire.

We need the outliers—those who are able to see the culture clearly—because most of us become so used to the status quo that we don't even notice it. We become *acclimated* and then *acculturated*. The concept of acclimation suggests that any environment can be eventually ignored. To illustrate, a person who lives close to the equator may claim that when it is 60 degrees outside it is cold, whereas a person who lives closer to one of the poles may claim that 60 degrees is warm weather. If these two switched locations, after an initial adjustment period, they would become acclimated to the point that they would change their initial opinions about 60-degree weather. This process of acclimation—adapting to a new environment or situation—can happen with language dialects, food preferences, city noises, pace of work, or any other situational constant. We acclimate to our surroundings to the point where we only notice them when they change.

Acculturation—the gradual process by which we acquire the culture of a particular society or group—requires us to accept certain truths, to recognize the current climate as "home" and defend it. It is the culture that determines the climate; the climate eventually fades out of consciousness, until it is disrupted. Whatever brand of education a school is selling, new members will acclimate to it, then be acculturated so as not to notice or question it.

We have established that acting *with* a culture makes it stronger and rewards the actor. When a teacher yells at students and nothing is done to stop it, the culture will whisper to everyone that yelling is OK. Over time, yelling will be seen as a strategy that works for teachers, for support staff, for whenever students talk to an adult. When new teachers are unable to gain control of a class, they may seek help from a veteran teacher who yells at students. If a new teacher challenges the veteran teacher's suggestion, the new teacher risks becoming an outlier, unless he or she initiates a repair soon after.

This is when the new teacher must decide whether he or she is going to be part of this group, try to change it, or leave it. Most will take the path of fitting in, which further cements the culture. Others may see the culture as a poor fit for them and find a position elsewhere. For some, though, pushing back seems worth the cost. These are the teachers who may best be able to visualize a new reality for the group. These are the teachers who can see the culture that all the others are blind to.

If a principal wants to start brainstorming a new vision for the school, those who have been there the longest and have chosen to fit in may struggle to imagine a new place or story. They may have strong levels of commitment to the good old days. The outliers, by contrast, have been imagining a new place every day. The trick is to get them to share their ideas. One caveat, however: they cannot be the ones *selling* the ideas. Just as the producers or writers of a movie are rarely in front of the camera, the outliers who envision a better culture remain behind the scenes. And chances are, they like it that way. The best salespeople in the organization, using the current culture as the means to sell improvements, should be the people who fit within the norm and are respected by the masses. Most movements happen because the masses followed the first *follower*, not so much the leader. That first follower needs to be a "normal" person (Sivers, 2010). As more people gradually join in, a new normal becomes established, and those who choose not to become part of the movement are now on the outside looking in.

Engage in School Culture Change Thoughtfully, Not Fashionably

As the concept of school culture continues to attract attention, we find it becoming a bit overused. Citing culture as the foundation for every improvement does not make sense; some improvements are just minor adjustments. A sure red flag is using culture as a fashionable buzzword to sell new initiatives. To keep the concept of school culture from becoming the ad line for every new idea that comes around, we want to give school leaders permission to build a strong school with many positive traits *without* claiming that each trait defines their culture. School culture is resilient and doesn't bend to every new trait trying to get attention. Changing school culture is more than buying into a new idea; school culture is the personality of the school. Thus, there will be positive and negative features that define it, and none of these will be changed simply because someone proclaims it so. To maintain your priorities and ensure the change is sustainable, keep the following in mind.

One person cannot change a culture alone. Cultures cannot exist with just one person. Even if that person has powerful charisma, the culture does nothing new when one leader stands alone. To lead a culture change, the person needs a small group of followers who have the ability to influence others without appearing to be trying to convince others. You cannot be the only one wanting the culture to change.

Changing the culture does not guarantee improvement. Because we are all human, with a wide array of imaginations, egos, temperaments, scars, and emotions, a recipe for what worked in one setting will not necessarily work somewhere else. One hundred people might use the same recipe to make a chocolate cake, but odds are no two cakes will taste exactly the same owing to variations in environment, cooking skill, equipment settings, and other factors. The same goes for any type of leadership initiative that attempts to emulate someone else's previous effort, whether it be Abraham Lincoln's or Gandhi's. Millions of copies of books recounting successful leadership and change efforts have been sold, yet how many of those millions of readers have replicated the success of those leaders? This does not mean you should not be inspired by others' efforts and try their powerful approaches; just don't be upset if your final work doesn't end up in a museum.

Sales pitches don't work. Most people can sense when you are trying to sell them something (Grenny et al., 2013). This awareness can scare away people who may have had above-average levels of commitment to the change initiative prior to hearing the leader glorify it like a used car salesperson. People have an instinct to recoil from anything that sounds more like a sales pitch than a conversation. If your vision for the future is one that your faculty truly aspires to, there will be no reason to invest much energy in selling it. It will sell itself.

Informal conversations trump formal announcements. School cultures are the way they are due to normal people in the school building going about their daily business with predictability and comfort. Much of what teachers choose to do throughout the day is laden with the values and beliefs of that school's culture. We are talking about the actions teachers take when they are free to act, most notably in the hallways before or after school or between classes, in the workroom, or during lunch. Whatever teachers talk about during informal conversations says more about the culture's values than any performance they give in the public eye.

When a strategy is not working, base changes on conditions, not personalities. When people are not performing well, it tends to be for one of two reasons: (1) they are unable to perform the work owing to insufficient training, or (2) they could do the job well but choose not to. Thus, we are left wondering why teachers who are trained and *could* do well seem to choose not to do well. Our response *should* be to check their role in the culture. It could be that their scripts don't fit the movie, or their capacities lie elsewhere. It's like Darth Vader showing up in *Winnie the Pooh*. Make sure you have not set up teachers for failure by putting them in a place that does not fit their strengths (see "Playing the Part: The Influence of Roles on School Culture" in Chapter 1).

The messenger shouldn't be more important than the message. How many people leave their churches because a beloved preacher has left? We can become enamored with the personalities of others to the point where interacting with those people becomes more rewarding than doing the job. We can train people

to need external motivation simply to do their jobs. We can create a history of rituals and routines that build dependence upon
emotional speeches rather than executing the mission. Watch what
happens to a school when an adored principal leaves. Schools that
lack a unity of purpose will collapse. Remember, as we discussed
in Chapter 2: it's important not to let personalities ride roughshod
over ideas.

Culture change takes time, but not much work. This may
sound strange, but school leaders should not be doing the heavy
lifting to change the culture of their schools. Leaders should be
planting seeds, creating conditions, and watching. Much of the
"work" should be accomplished by those who have been identified
as respected and connected. You will have a few strong teachers who
represent the future of your school. These are the people who should
be doing most of the work. Fortunately, they usually want to.

For a culture to change, it must be weakened. In this case,
weakened does not mean made worse or ineffective. It simply means
that some values and beliefs need to be challenged. Some beliefs
have been around a long time and have become a part of "who we
are around here." These beliefs make a culture strong. Remember,
strong doesn't necessarily equal *good;* a strong culture is simply one
that is difficult to change.

In *School Culture Rewired* (Gruenert & Whitaker, 2015), we discussed "culture busters," or ideas that can be used to lay bare the
current culture, making it vulnerable to change. However, exposing
the culture in such a way does not guarantee it will move to a more
positive place. It will remain vulnerable to change for a period of
time as the group looks for stasis. As the dust settles, leaders can
put pieces back into different places—like moving chess pieces in

the middle of a match when the opponent is not paying attention. Stirring things up just for the sake of it accomplishes nothing, however. It's crucial to have a long-term plan in mind before exposing a culture in this way.

We simply ask for leaders to weaken the culture by bringing to the table the values and beliefs that seem to be holding back progress. It won't tank test scores or drive the best teachers to bolt. In fact, these moves tend to build trust within the more effective tribes of teachers as they begin to realize what is happening.

If you cannot explain school culture to a 6th grader, you do not understand it well enough. Chances are you will never *need* to explain school culture to a 6th grader, but give it a try anyway. Grab a few kids during lunch and share your ideas with them. If you find it difficult to explain to them without using jargon from a leadership book—or using the word *culture*—then you have more learning to do to fully internalize the concept.

Avoid Rapid Culture Change

In this era of one-click shopping and voice assistants, we as a society are choosing to move faster than past generations, aided by technology. We are getting more done faster, which gives us time to do still more. Given this pace of life, could cultures also change at a faster pace? Is there merit in people's claims that they changed their organizational cultures in less than six months?

Simply put, no. As we discussed in Chapter 2, too much, too soon, is a recipe for disaster. As the old adage goes, a little learning is a dangerous thing. Too often, we hear about leaders who, with a seminar about culture change under their belts, attempt to launch an all-out campaign to transform their school's culture. If your goal is sustained school culture change, there is a pace at which your culture will tolerate you messing around with it. Go too fast, and the culture will eat you and your strategy.

Cultures are based on collective beliefs. Thus, when we change a culture, we are changing beliefs. Products that promise quick transformation abound in every arena—see, for example, spray tans, muscle-building pills, instant credit, and CliffsNotes. Can people be convinced their lives are unfulfilled and that a charismatic leader has the solution? That would be the essence of how a culture might be changed quickly, barring a traumatic event. But that quick change would not go deep. To change a culture, you need to change minds. Changing your mind is, in essence, learning. If you go too fast, you run the risk of ending up with one of the following two culture types.

The synthetic culture. Here we have a group that has come together to meet a temporary need. This temporary need may have been put in place by a person, system, or structure designed to sell a product or an idea. A synthetic culture is often fad-driven, based on a need that someone else has manufactured as a means for motivating certain behaviors. In schools this might be one of the following:

- The need to get all students to pass a test
- The need for the school to be everything for everyone
- The need to hide mistakes
- The need to constantly change
- The need to be defensive in light of criticism

Each of these needs, along with many others, creates a set of beliefs that can derail a good school. Over time, people may begin to believe that certain negative behaviors actually have benefits. A synthetic culture will not last very long, but the thinking it causes might make future synthetic cultures more possible, and it could prevent a positive culture from developing.

The virtual culture. In our current society, we have many places we can go virtually. The internet enables us to travel the world, have conversations with strangers, and instantly buy pretty much anything we want. It abounds with online forums connecting people with similar beliefs, preferences, life situations, or interests, such as fishing or psychedelic rock. It's not hard to become obsessed with what happens online. Given enough support, we can feel as though we are part of a family made up of people whom we have never met. People dedicate a lot of energy and emotions to some websites, perhaps looking for their next soulmate, and there are those who are waiting to "catfish" those people into relationships designed to fulfill ulterior motives.

The application of this phenomenon to schools and, more specifically, to school leaders will become more noticeable as each new generation of teachers arrives in August. Our newest teachers have been raised to keep a close eye on the internet as well as their cell phones. Given this shift, it is possible that the next generation of teachers will value relationships that form virtually as much as those formed in the school building. The school culture may splinter because a greater proportion of teachers are more deeply immersed in external virtual cultures, which provide instant connection and are easy to navigate and feel a part of, than they are in their day-to-day school cultures, which don't allow them to conveniently gloss over obstacles and differences. Loyalty to the work family may diminish as the list of virtual families grows.

Summing Up

To wrap up this chapter and get you started on your culture change journey, we'd like to provide a recap of obstacles to look out for and where to focus your efforts.

Factors that work against your change efforts may include the following:

- **Past leadership hanging around.** This could be the guy who wants to return to the classroom for a few years before retiring. This person could be the one people run to when the new leader makes a mistake.
- **Past leadership legacies.** The past leader may have been there for 30 years and even have a plaque or statue in front of the building. This era could become the standard by which all future leaders will be judged.
- **Your own legacy.** If you have risen from assistant principal to principal after a long tenure at your school, it is unlikely that anything new will be brought to the table. Anyone who has been at a school for more than five years is part of the culture and may not be able to see a different one—*unless* that person is willing to look in the mirror with a critical eye. By surrounding ourselves with outliers who represent the most effective educators and remaining open to new ideas, we can correct for our own blindness to the culture.
- **Longtime toxic staffers.** As we've outlined in this chapter, transferring influence from your toxic staff to your new or better teachers offers an avenue for sustained change. Divide and conquer the toxic ones, not the effective ones.
- **Past successes.** This is the main ingredient of a closed mindset. Having a reputation as a great school can freeze some values and beliefs for perpetuity and deter changes in the future.

- **Trends and fads.** Go ahead and get excited at conferences, but make sure the latest trends in culture change that you take away from the conferences really meet the unique needs of your school—and will do so for the foreseeable future—before upending the current culture.
- **A local definition of *normal*.** Average is a magnet. The mean is gravity, and the median is a boundary. Whatever happens all the time at your school is considered *normal,* and it is what attracts or repels new people, good or bad. Watch out for toxicity or even mediocrity becoming the new normal.

Make sure you're focusing on the following:

- **The best people.** Your best employees—especially your most effective teachers—should shape the future of your school. Changing the culture of a school is not as much an administrative, a student, or a community effort as it is a teacher thing.
- **Your expressed commitment.** It is important that people know where you stand as well as your passion for improvement, but not to the point that it makes others feel guilty or embarrassed as they grow toward a stronger commitment.
- **A mission that defines who you are and why you are here.** Your school mission shouldn't just be a checklist of what is on everyone's plate. The reason your teachers became teachers should be the reason they still come to school. If their personal mission is to make a difference in children's lives but all anyone talks about is testing, well, the misalignment is killing their spirits.
- **A vision that sounds like a movie everyone wants a role in.** Returning to our movie metaphor, the vision shouldn't just sound like a movie that would be fun to see. It needs to be

sweeping, with a place for everyone, and it should go deep. Aim for your school culture to be a movie that all have seen many times and love. Teachers should not be allowed to criticize the movie because, like it or not, they are actors in the movie. Instead, give teachers permission to change their roles if they see a better outcome.

- **Past successes.** Having a history of success can be a block to changes in the future, but it can also indicate that past decisions have been good, meaning you may have at least some of the culture you want already in place. Past successes can also provide a strong foundation on which to build other areas of your culture that you'd like to change.

A Final Word

Your culture is telling a story. People are sharing it. Is it the story you want to be told?

If you want to navigate sustained school culture change, it is important to understand that culture is more about the informal conversations and stories that happen in the hallways between classes and among teachers than about any formal meeting with administration that proclaims a new mindset. It can be that simple—and yet that complex. These conversations need to happen at the right times, among the right people, saying the right things. We could provide a recipe with a calendar, a teacher selection process, and a script. But just like 100 people baking a cake using the same recipe, there are no guarantees that you will end up with what others have made. If anyone tries to sell you that guarantee, run.

Bruner (1997) tells us that culture is a way of knowing. Going beyond what we know means changing the culture. It means unlearning some knowledge, habits, and dispositions and redefining what is possible. This is the stuff our best teachers, our new teachers, and a few weirdos bring to the table. Their naivete and stubbornness become a strength. We cannot stress enough how much the culture is going to try and make them fit in. Get in front of that and don't let it happen.

School cultures should not be viewed as dysfunctional. Even at the worst schools, where we admit the culture is the problem, it is still doing its job (i.e., functioning) very well. For a culture to be dysfunctional, it would need to fail to influence people's beliefs, attitudes, or behaviors. There is always a culture driving any group of people who have spent a significant amount of time together serving a common purpose. Unfortunately, in some schools, this common purpose may be individual survival or teacher welfare. If the leaders do nothing, these schools will devolve into toxicity.

We hope this book gives leaders the confidence to change the cultures of their schools with the ultimate goal of improving student and teacher performance. What we have shared reflects our own experiences with schools and their leadership teams. We welcome opportunities to continue these discussions as we learn more about school culture.

Finally, we encourage you to take on this challenge if you believe your school's current culture is holding back your collective potential. Having the capacity to fix it obligates you to fix it. This effort will take a greater level of commitment than most realize. Our encounters with leaders who have succeeded have shown us that those who prevail are usually the ones who devoted a high enough level of passion and drive to see it through. If you are passionate about improving your school, then let that commitment be your superpower.

References

Bellah, R. N., Madsen, R., Sullivan, W. M., Swidler, A., & Tipton, S. M. (2007). *Habits of the heart: Individualism and commitment in American life*. Oakland, CA: University of California Press.

Bogue, E. G. (1985). *The enemies of leadership: Lessons for leaders in education*. Arlington, VA: Phi Delta Kappa International.

Bruner, J. (1997). *Toward a theory of instruction*. Cambridge, MA: Harvard University Press.

Cialdini, R. (2018). *Pre-suasion: A revolutionary way to influence and persuade*. New York: Simon & Schuster.

Deal, T. E., & Peterson, K. D. (2010). *Shaping school culture: Pitfalls, paradoxes, and promises*. New York: Wiley.

Geertz, C. (1973). *The interpretation of cultures*. New York: Basic Books.

Grenny, J., Patterson, K., Maxfield, D., McMillan, R., & Switzer, A. (2013). *Influencer: The new science of leading change* (2nd ed.). New York: McGraw-Hill.

Gruenert, S. W., & McDaniel, T. M. (2009, November). The making of a weak teacher: A preposterous notion about the role of administrators in crafting an unsupportive work environment. *School Administrator, 66*(10), 30–33.

Gruenert, S., & Whitaker, T. (2015). *School culture rewired: How to define, assess, and transform it*. Alexandria, VA: ASCD.

Gruenert, S., & Whitaker, T. (2017). *School culture recharged: Strategies to energize your staff and culture*. Alexandria, VA: ASCD.

Gruenert, S., & Whitaker, T. (2019). Manuscript in preparation.

Hall, E. (1990). *Beyond culture*. New York: Anchor Books.

Hanifan, L. J. (1916, September). The rural school community center. *The Annals of the American Academy of Political and Social Science, 67*, 130–138.

Hanson, M. (2009). *Collaboration: How leaders avoid the traps, build common ground, and reap big results*. Cambridge, MA: Harvard Business Review Press.

Hofstede, G., Hofstede, G. J., & Minkov, M. (2010). *Cultures and organizations: Software of the mind: Intercultural cooperation and its importance for survival* (3rd ed.). New York: McGraw-Hill.

Louni, A., & Subbalakshmi, K. P. (2014). Diffusion of information in social networks. In M. Panda, S. Dehuri, & G. N. Wang (Eds.), *Social networking: Intelligent systems reference library* (Vol. 65, pp. 1–22). Switzerland: Springer.

Potter, R., & Hastings, W. (2004). *Trust me: Developing a leadership style people will follow.* Ann Arbor, MI: Archigia Press.

Schein, E. H., with Schein, P. (2017). *Organizational culture and leadership* (5th ed.). Hoboken, NJ: Wiley.

Sivers, D. (2010, April 4). *TED Talk: How to start a movement* [Video]. Retrieved March 3, 2019, from https://www.ted.com/talks/derek_sivers_how_to_start_a_movement

Index

Note: Page references followed by an italicized *f* indicate information contained in figures.

About the Authors

Steve Gruenert is a professor at Indiana State University. He has studied organizational culture and climate for more than 20 years and continues to learn and collaborate with other researchers as these concepts evolve. He is coauthor, with Todd Whitaker, of *School Culture Rewired: How to Define, Assess, and Transform It* (ASCD) and *School Culture Recharged: Strategies to Energize Your Staff and Culture* (ASCD), and, with Ryan Donlan, of *Minds Unleashed: How Principals Can Lead the Right-Brained Way* (Rowman & Littlefield). He and his wife, Emily, have three daughters: Jennifer, Mackenzi, and Madison. He can be reached at steve.gruenert@indstate.edu.

Todd Whitaker is fortunate to have been able to blend his passion with his career. He is a leading presenter in the field of education and a professor of educational leadership at the University of Missouri and professor emeritus at Indiana State University. He has previously served as both a teacher and a principal and is the author of over 40 books, including *What Great Teachers Do Differently, Your First Year,* and *Shifting the Monkey,* along with the books he has coauthored with Steve Gruenert. Whitaker and his wife, Beth, have three children: Katherine, Madeline, and Harrison.

Related ASCD Resources

At the time of publication, the following resources were available (ASCD stock numbers appear in parentheses).

Print Products

100+ Ways to Recognize and Reward Your School Staff by Emily E. Houck (#112051)

Dream Team: A Practical Playbook to Help Innovative Educators Change Schools by Aaron Tait and Dave Faulkner (#119022)

How to Create a Culture of Achievement in Your School and Classroom by Douglas Fisher, Nancy Frey, and Ian Pumpian (#111014)

The Principal 50: Critical Leadership Questions for Inspiring Schoolwide Excellence by Baruti K. Kafele (#115050)

School Climate Change: How do I build a positive environment for learning? (ASCD Arias) by Peter DeWitt and Sean Slade (#SF114084)

School Culture Recharged: Strategies to Energize Your Staff and Culture by Steve Gruenert and Todd Whitaker (#117016)

School Culture Rewired: How to Define, Assess, and Transform It by Steve Gruenert and Todd Whitaker (#115004)

For up-to-date information about ASCD resources, go to www.ascd.org. You can search the complete archives of *Educational Leadership* at www.ascd.org/el.

ASCD myTeachSource®

Download resources from a professional learning platform with hundreds of research-based best practices and tools for your classroom at http://myteachsource.ascd.org/.

For more information, send an e-mail to member@ascd.org; call 1-800-933-2723 or 703-578-9600; send a fax to 703-575-5400; or write to Information Services, ASCD, 1703 N. Beauregard St., Alexandria, VA 22311-1714 USA.

The ASCD Whole Child approach is an effort to transition from a focus on narrowly defined academic achievement to one that promotes the long-term development and success of all children. Through this approach, ASCD supports educators, families, community members, and policymakers as they move from a vision about educating the whole child to sustainable, collaborative actions.

Committing to the Culture relates to the **engaged, supported**, and **challenged** tenets. *For more about the ASCD Whole Child approach, visit* **www.ascd.org/wholechild.**

WHOLE CHILD
TENETS

1 HEALTHY
Each student enters school healthy and learns about and practices a healthy lifestyle.

2 SAFE
Each student learns in an environment that is physically and emotionally safe for students and adults.

3 ENGAGED
Each student is actively engaged in learning and is connected to the school and broader community.

4 SUPPORTED
Each student has access to personalized learning and is supported by qualified, caring adults.

5 CHALLENGED
Each student is challenged academically and prepared for success in college or further study and for employment and participation in a global environment.